ADVANCE P[
LOVE IS AN INSIDE JOB

"This book is a beautiful reminder from a man who weaves his love for Jesus with real talk about vulnerability in a way that everyone can relate to and learn from. Romal kicks the doors of complacency open wide and, with arms outstretched, invites us to enter into wholeness."

—Bob Goff, author of *Love Does: Discover a Secretly Incredible Life in an Ordinary World*

"I love books that fully engage you from the first page—with deep humanity, dear honesty, and yes vulnerability! Books like this. I fear that I write far too abstractly and theoretically compared to Romal Tune. Read and meet a man on the real journey. It will change the way you see life, death, and perhaps even God."

—Fr. Richard Rohr, O.F.M., author of *Falling Upward* and *Breathing Under Water*

"All of us face challenges as we seek to live lives of purpose and meaning, but Romal Tune has faced more than his share. Every story in this book says, 'There's a way through'—if you are willing to do hard inner work and give yourself to God's love. For those in search of inner peace and deeper meaning, this book will serve as a guide and a sign of hope."

—Parker J. Palmer, author of *Let Your Life Speak, The Courage to Teach,* and *On the Brink of Everything*

"I found Romal Tune's book riveting, real, and relevant to anyone who wants to live their best life and who knows that requires doing the work to heal from the wounds inflicted along the way. Romal is honest about his wins, his losses, and what he is doing to improve and shows us what we all can do to improve. He is going to help a lot of people with this work."

—Brian Courtney Wilson, Grammy Nominated Singer/Songwriter/Recording Artist

"A resounding thanks to Romal Tune for reminding me once again that vulnerability is one of our greatest superpowers! *Love Is an Inside Job* is an emancipating message for those of us searching for a deeper, more authentic relationship with ourselves, the calling on our lives, and, yes, with God. Through the lens of Tune's life lessons, this book shows what true, unconditional love can look like for all of us."

—Shawn Dove, CEO, Campaign for Black Male Achievement

LOVE
IS AN
INSIDE
JOB

LOVE IS AN INSIDE JOB

Getting Vulnerable with God

ROMAL TUNE

FaithWords

New York Nashville

FaithWords
Hachette Book Group
1290 Avenue of the Americas, New York, NY 10104
faithwords.com
twitter.com/faithwords

First Edition: April 2018

FaithWords is a division of Hachette Book Group, Inc. The FaithWords name and logo are trademarks of Hachette Book Group, Inc.

The publisher is not responsible for websites (or their content) that are not owned by the publisher.

The Hachette Speakers Bureau provides a wide range of authors for speaking events. To find out more, go to www.hachettespeakersbureau.com or call (866) 376-6591.

Library of Congress Cataloging-in-Publication Data has been applied for.

ISBNs: 978-1-4789-9260-8 (trade paperback), 978-1-4789-9259-2 (ebook)

Printed in the United States of America

LSC-C

10 9 8 7 6 5 4 3 2 1

To God—the power of love, the freedom of forgiveness. Thank you for the reciprocity of vulnerability and the blessing of unmerited grace.

Contents

INTRODUCTION
To Love Thy Neighbor as Thyself, Get Vulnerable with God

Master, which is the great commandment in the law? Jesus said unto him, Thou shalt love the Lord thy God with all thy heart, and with all thy soul, and with all thy mind. This is the first and great commandment. And the second is like unto it, Thou shalt love thy neighbor as thyself.

Matthew 22:36–40 KJV

My follow-up question after Jesus explained the greatest commandment went something like this: "How do I love my neighbor when I don't love myself?" What I felt for myself was shame about a past that haunted me—guilt and fear—not self-love. I loved others if they loved me first. If they loved me, I'd have reason to love myself.

Loving God with my "all"—with my whole self—

meant going all in. I didn't go all in for anything. I didn't totally trust or show all my feelings to anyone. Sermons I heard in church talked about the things God gives to those God loves, so if I received what I wanted, then God loved me and I'd love God back. God and I were cool. But when life wasn't going my way, that meant God had let me down, abandoned me, like everyone else who was supposed to love me unconditionally. God and I were distant. I was used to disappointment, so I could handle God not loving me. No sweat.

My love for God and my love for people was cautious love. I kept up a wall. I didn't let down my guard. In every case in my life—from family, to friends, to marriage, to church, I had been somehow disappointed. I wasn't willing to risk being let down or hurt again.

This book is about how I moved from my idea of being loved by God based on what God did for me, to experiencing God's unconditional love for me, which helped me love myself and love others. I wanted to be a better person, experience peace of mind, and overcome my constant fear of never being enough for myself, God, or anyone else. Discovering the power of vulnerability opened the door for me to become the person I truly desired to be and live the life I have always wanted—a life free from anxiety, dread of the future, fear of failure, and loneliness. Learning that love starts *inside* me—with vulnerability to God—has given me a new sense of freedom. The route to that most profound relationship with God was vulnerability. Receiving God's love meant being vulnerable with God. Loving God meant being vulnerable with God. In vulnerability with God, I discovered self-love. From self-love, my relationships have been transformed.

I've carried a lot of emotional baggage my whole life. My baggage was not the kind you can carry on a flight and place in an overhead bin. Mine was like the baggage you place on the scale at the check-in counter and you hear the clerk say: "Your baggage is over the weight limit and you're going to have to pay for that." Yes, my baggage has been heavy and I've paid dearly in inner pain, fractured relationships, and life drama. For a long time, I knew it was over the weight limit but I carried it anyway. I thought I needed it for my manhood, the person I wanted to show the world, and I paid a high price. The cost was my peace of mind, happiness, friendships, and loss of those I loved.

Throughout this book, I will shares stories from my

past that I finally had to confront on my journey to embracing the love of God, the love of myself, and the ability to love others. This is about the oftentimes complicated road to redemption, forgiveness, and the need for grace. My hope is that as you read this book, you will be able to glean lessons and tools from my mistakes as well as my healing that will be useful to you on your own journey to become the best version of yourself that you can possibly become in your lifetime. Love is an inside job, and sometimes your secrets are the source of your sorrows. Doing the inner work allows you to confront your secrets and overcome the root source of your sadness. My prayer is for everyone who reads this book to embrace the love of God, the love of self, and the love of others in order to live your life free of guilt or shame. Live without internal turmoil. Live with peace of mind knowing that you are already amazing and you don't have to prove it.

When I say, "Love is an inside job," I'm saying love can be experienced only from the inside. Inner love never fades, and you never have to question it. That love isn't emotional; it's spiritual. God is the source of love, and when you embrace the love of God, you are able to love yourself and then love others. It flows from the inside out.

My inability to accept love or genuinely offer it to anyone else was due to challenging and sometimes traumatic life experiences. While parts of me kept up a front, running from my past, hiding my pain, and fearing shame, my soul yearned to be free from what haunted me and to experience the elusive love I'd been searching for. I had to unpack the baggage. I had to remember, re-examine, and finally resolve the stories that had been weighing me down. Dealing with the experiences that created my life-limiting be-liefs was an inside job. My healing work was long overdue. In this book I am sharing my journey, my story, as an invitation to take a serious look at yours. I invite you to get to the source of your life-limiting beliefs, doubts, fears, and negative views you harbor about yourself. Unapologetically begin to love every aspect of the amazing person that you were created to be.

All thy heart, *all* thy soul, *all* thy mind meant going all-in with God; it meant being vulnerable with God, and only that vulnerability produced self-love. There is no way to truly love people without first loving self and no way to truly love self without God, Who is the source of love. The love of God leads to the love of self and results in the love of others:

Love of God > Self-Love > Love of Others

I tend to be a giving and generous person who is there for others when they are in need of support. My motives for generosity and empathy were not a genuine outflow of God's love. I donated money to help kids go to college. I volunteered to help friends with work and personal projects, told my story of overcoming childhood challenges at gatherings for teens coming out of juvenile detention, spoke at prisons to inmates who were parents, and so on. I did good in order to be loved, rather than as a genuine expression of love without a hidden agenda. I was motivated by my desire for control. I was unwilling to let go and fully let God in. And for good reason. I needed to remain in control because if I did not take things into my own hands, I would not be okay because no one was going to help me, not even God.

But finally, I got tired.

Richard Rohr calls this feeling dehydration. He names the replenishing that prevents dehydration "the feeling of full flow, vulnerability, and trust in the infilling." The willingness to let go of control and admit the desire to love and be loved can only be found through letting in the love of God first. This "inflow" of love prevents "dehydration."

My inability to embrace the inflow has led to many broken relationships. Whenever I became dehydrated, I gave up. I was empty and had nothing more to give. So many mistakes and fractured relationships have been the result of my inability to let love in. My way was "love your neighbor, *then* yourself." That's like turning on a faucet and having the water shoot up into your face, creating a mess.

I had to learn that the love of God, which results in the love of self and then neighbor, *begins* with vulnerability. It was impossible to love my neighbor as myself when I didn't know how to love myself first. I couldn't love myself without experiencing God's love, and I couldn't experience God's love for me without being vulnerable.

Vulnerability is the birthplace of love, belonging, joy, courage, empathy, and creativity. It is the source of hope, empathy, accountability, and authenticity. If we want greater clarity in our purpose or deeper and more meaningful spiritual lives, vulnerability is the path.

Brené Brown

These words from Brené Brown's *Daring Greatly: How the Courage to Be Vulnerable Transforms the Way We Live, Love, Parent, and Lead* were the opening quote in one of Richard's daily meditations. The thought of vulnerability frustrated me. I didn't want to be vulnerable. I was afraid of it. I believed that vulnerability led to pain.

But I was wrong. That's not always the case. When I began to explore the outcomes of my life as a result of my unwillingness to be vulnerable, I realized how much it was causing me to remain disconnected from people. Therapy helped me to start seeing the value of vulnerability and the opportunity for deeper relationships that it offers. Vulnerability is the only way to receive love and in turn extend love to others. I learned that vulnerability is the path to truly experiencing the love of God and finally love the person I am.

I had no examples of going all in with God, being vulnerable with God.

I had no examples of self-love.

I didn't even know where to start in order to give vulnerability a try. Control was my way of dealing. When I got tired, I wanted to become vulnerable, but it was not easy.

This book shares my story and process of embracing vulnerability:

Vulnerability with God > Love of God > Self-Love > Love of Others

CHAPTER 1

"When the Parts of Me I Didn't Love Led a Revolt"

When you don't love all of who you are, the parts you don't love will lead a revolt.

Phil Jackson, founder and lead pastor, House Covenant Church, Chicago, Illinois

I was an urban outreach minister sitting in the church office one beautiful Sunday morning, preparing for service at this megachurch of five thousand members, when one of the deacons came running in.

"A homeless man is threatening people in the kitchen!"

He'd bypassed other congregational leaders, perhaps figuring this was a situation for the "urban outreach" minister to handle.

Rather than serving the homeless in other locations, we had started bringing displaced persons to church to worship with us and have breakfast with us, truly becoming a part of the church community. Imagine middle-class, upper-middle-class, even wealthy people, and homeless ones, all having breakfast. It was awkward at times. The homeless man was a regular in our food program, whom I now remember as Mr. Breakfast. He was a slender man, perhaps fifty years old, six feet tall, with a short scruffy beard, wearing a baseball cap and a tattered green coat and jeans. He was carrying four bags of food that smelled distinctly like bacon. When I approached him and asked, "Why are you taking food? We will give you all you can eat," he responded, "What are you talking about, Rev? I gotta feed my family."

I was responsible for pastoral care and outreach, so this wasn't my first interaction with this man. I knew him. We had been engaging him for months. Trying to keep it one hundred with him, I said, "Look, man, you don't have to lie to me. You know you don't have family."

I knew for sure he didn't have family, but he got angry: "So what are you going to do, Rev?"

I was standing there in a preacher's robe adorned with velvet crosses, hardly a year out of divinity. Mr. Breakfast and I were in view of members who were business professionals, doctors, and lawyers, entering a church that had been visited by every president who came to the city. I had been in situations like this during my teenage years but never with a homeless person, so when Mr. Breakfast squared off in front of me, I knew exactly what to do. I sat my coffee down on the ledge of a flowerbed, preparing to control what might happen.

Mr. Breakfast asked again, "What are you going to do, Rev?"

The thought did occur to me: *Maybe I should pray for him, or maybe if this gets physical, I'll just turn the other cheek*, and then I heard him say, "I'll slap you!"

Mr. Breakfast and I were about to fight. My actions had quickly vetoed the idea of turning the other cheek.

A short elderly man in his seventies, wearing glasses and a hat that said CHURCH SECURITY, and a group of guys from the congregation restrained me.

Mr. Breakfast was sent back to the streets. I was taken to the pastor's office and reprimanded.

"Things just got real," I explained to the senior pastor. "There was no way I could allow myself to be slapped by Mr. Breakfast, a homeless man—in church, on Sunday morning!" All of my hard-earned street credibility would be lost in an instant!

"Romal, you're wearing a robe with velvet crosses on it," he reminded me, as if I didn't realize I was still draped in the robe. "Why didn't you let church security handle it?"

"When I saw a man who looked to be in his mid-seventies walking up with his church security hat on," I told him, "my initial thought was, *Great. I have to protect both of us now!*"

Pastor reminded me of my work bringing the homeless into community within our church, how I'd talked about how loving our neighbors as ourselves was the underpinning of bringing the church soup kitchen into the church cafeteria. He said I couldn't love that homeless man, because I didn't know how to love myself. What was inside me was the street Romal preserving self via the way of the street, not the loved-by-God Romal who was self-loving enough to choose other ways to handle Mr. Breakfast.

The pastor sent me to anger management.

My altercation with Mr. Breakfast turned out to be a blessing in disguise. Counseling began a process of healing old wounds. What Mr. Breakfast said and did raised deep-seated inner issues in me and about my past. I was conflicted inside. The parts of me that I didn't like, parts that had led me to the urban ministry job in the first place, had resurfaced in unhealthy ways. I thought I could resolve my inner conflicts by serving in the church, praying, worshipping, leaning on my newly found, nonviolent Christian values, but the incident with Mr. Breakfast proved I needed help.

CHAPTER 2

The Verdict Was Therapy

A wise Senior Pastor at the church where I worked while a student in Seminary said to me, "Jorge, you're a gifted leader but your unresolved issues will destroy your life and ministry. Get help or I'll fire you." Thus began my thirty-plus-year relationship with skilled counselors who have helped me navigate through the wreckage and beauty of my life. God uses counselors and other mental health professionals to bring about His sanctifying grace in our lives.

Jorge Acevedo, lead pastor, Grace Church,
Cape Coral, Florida

Getting sent to anger management was my first shot at therapy. It felt like punishment. It came with stigmas. What will other people think of me? Yes, I was angry.

Yes, places in my life were causing me pain, but nobody knew. Now I worried about what people would think. I wanted to protect the public perception of me, even if that perception wasn't true. Other people's opinions of me were more important than my own well-being. I treated my life like a Facebook post—talked only about all the good—because I wanted people to think my life was great, even though I knew for myself that wasn't true. I wasn't as happy as I looked in those pictures I posted on Facebook. I pretended to be happy, not knowing how to actually be happy.

And no, I didn't want to talk about it.

I was "doing church" just fine. If church members knew I was in therapy, they might whisper that my "spirit was not right." If they knew I was going to therapy, they might tell me, "Just read the Bible. Something must be wrong with your prayer life. Jesus will break the yoke. You just need an 'anointing.' You don't need to go to therapy." None of which would help me deal with the life events that were the source of the problem. It was not my spirit but the stories—painful childhood life events—that were the source of my anger.

I am a man. I felt I could just deal with it myself, whatever "it" was. I can carry it; I can fix it myself. As a man, I was supposed to "man up." A man stands on his own two feet, makes his own decisions. A man fixes things himself. A man, a strong man, a real man, does not go to therapy.

I first went to therapy mainly because I had to go, but there was also a part of me that wanted to feel whole. I told myself that as a man, I could decide for myself to embrace it and not care what others thought. I had given my life to Christ because I wanted peace of mind and to be happy, yet something always made me anxious and afraid. Every time I got in a good situation, my mind made things go wrong. Mr. Breakfast hadn't started the fight. My thoughts had started the fight. My mind took me back to the streets, when I was actually in a situation far removed from my past. I was trapped by who I was told I could become in the world, by my own assumptions about who I was in the world. Instead of being who I was in the present—a minister—I acted out who I had been in my past—a scared boy from the inner city who always had to fight to survive, the skinny kid who was taught to throw the first punch.

WHY MEN DON'T GO TO THERAPY

The first question I had to ask myself when my pastor sentenced me to anger management was *Why don't men go to therapy?* I started asking my male friends about therapy and why men don't go. They told me men don't go to therapy because if you do, you are perceived by other men *and* women as weak, and perhaps you even think of yourself as weak. My own feelings were corroborated when they said another reason men don't go to therapy is because of the shame that comes with letting people know that something is wrong or that there are things you can't figure out or handle yourself.

As I struggled with these feelings and beliefs about therapy, this question kept popping into my head: What is the value of being strong if your definition of "being strong" results in pain because you keep breaking things, because you don't know how to change your behavior?

As a man, I have to be viewed as strong. That is what I'd been taught from the time I was a kid. I had accepted it as true. But until that pastor-mandated therapy, I never questioned the whole idea. What is real strength? What does it mean to be strong? I had been taught that being strong means that you handle things, that you deal with things on your own, that you fix things, that you figure them out, that you do not ask for help.

As I faced the prospect of going to therapy, I had to admit to myself that my idea of strength left out a lot. My uncles only taught me to be strong—a fighter—but nowhere along the way did I learn the value of empathy, compassion, affection, and love. I didn't know what empathy, compassion, affection, and love looked like coming from a strong man. Could I be a man who has the ability to be firm but also at the same time be compassionate, loving, caring, empathetic, and understanding? Would it bring into question my manhood or my strength? Deep inside, I wanted to be strong *and* be a man able to embrace all these aspects of myself. But I didn't know how.

I'd been taught that a man stands on his own two feet and makes his own decisions. My uncles would tell me that following anything my friends wanted to do was a sign of being a weak man. They never asked anyone for help when going through life's challenges, so I learned from their example and accepted their advice. As I faced that first prospect of therapy, I asked myself: If I'm a man who makes my own decisions, shouldn't I be able to choose therapy? If I'm a man who fixes things when they are wrong or going wrong, shouldn't I see myself as a man when I go to therapy to learn how to fix things in my life, especially when what needs to be fixed is me? Isn't deciding to go to therapy *evidence* that I am a man, a strong man?

Saying I could "just fix it myself" was like handling

shattered glass. The hidden parts of myself were like broken pieces with sharp edges, and every time I tried to reassemble them, I cut myself. Eventually I would hurt others. Yet, as a man, I could not ask for help.

So, at first I was resistant to my pastor's order that I go to therapy, but as I began to examine myself—my real self, not the person I wanted people to think I was, who had that great "carefully filtered half-truth posted on Facebook"—I began to question what I had accepted as true about myself because of my past. I could no longer accept those old ideas of manhood as true. Accepting the belief about manhood that I inherited from my family as true had become harmful to me; they were preventing me from becoming the person I truly wanted to be. Those ideas of what it meant to be a man no longer had value to me. Those beliefs about my manhood no longer served me well. Being a man with those beliefs that I had accepted without questioning kept causing me to harm not only myself but also others.

As I became less reluctant about going to therapy, one friend said, "Man, why do you need someone else to tell you what to do?" It suggested that I was either weak or not in control. My knee-jerk reaction was to continue putting forth the image, the persona that I can handle things, that I am in control, and I will hide the reality that I can't handle things. No one has to know that on the inside I'm falling apart. But after our conversation, my questions to myself were: What is the value of maintaining a perception that isn't accurate and keeps you from becoming the person you are supposed to be? I faced the truth that the perception I'd worked so hard to maintain kept me from peace of mind and happiness. Was what I wanted people to think of me worth the price of not having joy, not having peace? Was that perception worth the price of the inner pain that I endured? Sacrificing true happiness on the altar of public perception was no longer worth the price I was paying. I was tired of carrying burdens that erupted in anger and fighting because I was so concerned with what people thought of me.

The pursuit of pleasing people with a false identity for the sake of public perception was exhausting. I finally got tired of performing and worrying about what other people will think. Some part of me cared more about having peace than maintaining the perception that I was in control. For years I pretended to be happy, pretended that I enjoyed life, but now I actually wanted to become the person I was pretending to be.

It was with great discomfort and anxiety that I let go of who I wanted people to think I was. Pastor had blown my cover. Little did I know at the time that his mandated therapy would give me tools to not only love myself but genuinely love others and feel confident in who I am.

WHY BLACK FOLKS DON'T GO TO THERAPY

Although my pastor was black and the church was a historic black megachurch, full of the well educated, I saw that, regardless of social standing, African Americans generally don't go to therapy. Counseling was not openly talked about in my church community. It is often viewed as something that's for rich white people or—for those where I grew up—a last resort to avoid going to jail. I had a cousin who was given the option of jail time or mental health counseling. He chose the counseling. But then I thought about the many ways African Americans have been traumatized in Western culture—slavery, economics, social and political oppression, fighting for equality and equity, challenges of poverty, mass incarceration, educational disparities, and on and on—and I felt it was only natural that we all would need therapy!

Most acknowledge the violence that is perpetuated against people of color, African Americans specifically, but we don't acknowledge the psychological and emotional violence meted out to us now and over the centuries. Yet African Americans don't go to therapy, because we assume that if you do, something is wrong with you—you must be crazy or mentally ill. Going to therapy suggests that you just can't handle our oppression, as if to endure it is a racial badge of honor. I've learned that fighting for social and economic equality doesn't necessarily mean that it will liberate you from the mental and emotional impact of what you've been through. That requires a different kind of fight. It's an internal battle, an inside job.

I had tried carrying the weight of all the hell I'd been through and just living as if it were not that heavy, ignoring the burden of my own past and of history. I pursued success, thinking, More money, more things, more prestige would eventually fix my life. That didn't work and I knew it because, even robed up as a minister with two degrees, having graduated at the top of my class twice and having served in the military, I still showed who I was—an easily provoked black man off the streets. I lived the idea that all of my problems were behind me now and life would be good if I just did everything for myself. And I did it. I got a college education; I bought the right stuff—homes, cars, tailor-

made suits—and had the success persona. Yet I knew
these things, my accomplishments, had not delivered
on the promise. I still was not happy. I only pretended
to be happy. So, I had to ask: What is going to make me
happy? Can therapy help me find out?

When I thought about therapy, the stigma it carries
in my community, as well as in other cultural contexts—
the assumption of weakness and not being able to
handle oppression—I had to make a choice. Just as I had
to examine what I believed about being a man, I had
to re-examine my own ideas of blackness and struggle.
Why do I just have to *handle* oppression? Why do I
have to just carry the burden and suck it up without
admitting that carrying it, sucking it up, and enduring it
hurt me? Why do I need to feel ashamed that my success
has failed to heal centuries of oppression? Who is my
real community and could this pastor who says I have to
go to therapy be part of it?

Believing myths about therapy were not helping me,
and as I looked squarely at the stigmas against therapy,
I understood they were unfounded. I began to talk to
highly functioning people I knew whose happiness was
real, not just appearing to be real—people who had internal peace that was aligned with their external
happiness. They told me they actually go to therapy!

One friend—an African American male in his fifties—told me, "It allows me to sit in the presence of someone and talk about the challenges I am dealing with and find a new way forward." When asked whether he went to therapy on his own or, like me, was forced to go, another friend nodded with a yes—affirming that he saw a therapist—and said, "It helps me understand myself emotionally better. It teaches me how to become a better person."

A rule in broader African American culture and especially black churches is we don't tell people our business; we don't put our mess in the street. "What goes on in this house stays in this house." Gossip was behind the idea of not telling anyone your business, and given all the gossip that goes on in churches, I understood the roots of this caution. But my fears were put to rest when I was told: "It allows you to get it out in a safe place, where you know it will never be repeated. When you get it out, when you speak it, it takes the weight off."

What we've had to go through as a people has an impact on the consciousness and subconsciousness of even the most highly functioning African Americans and how we feel about ourselves. As a black male, I am aware every single day that the moment I walk out of my house, it is highly possible that I will have to deal with some form of discrimination or assumption about me because of the color of my skin. That has an impact. I have to constantly fight against that psychologically and mentally.

By mandating therapy, my pastor was challenging stigmas in African American culture that prevent me from being unapologetically and authentically myself, standing up for my truth, and not letting cultural barriers stand in the way of my emotional health. He forced me to examine the aspects of black culture that needed to be questioned and caused me to start asking myself: What is the value of beliefs and stigmas that keep me unhealthy? Rather than being "black enough" to withstand oppression, shouldn't my community and my culture be proud of me for doing what I need to do in order to be healthy, feel happy, have peace, show compassion, and display affection and love? Shouldn't my community be proud of me for doing what it takes to become the best person I can be and to live that way courageously and boldly?

WHY CHRISTIANS DON'T GO TO THERAPY

While my pastor was challenging the stigmas of therapy in African American culture, the church was another matter. I didn't grow up in the church. I had very limited interaction with church during my childhood and didn't become a believer until I was twenty-four years old. A lot about church I didn't know. Even after I've been a part of the church community for the last twenty years, much remains that I don't understand about how and why people "do church." I ran smack into some church culture norms regarding therapy.

In my experience, I have observed that church people regard emotional or mental health as a spiritual issue. If you are not emotionally healthy, something is wrong with your prayer life, your spirituality, or your faith.

Fortunately, I had never bought into that. My view was, if my emotional or psychological challenges are related to something that happened to me—verbal, physical, sexual, or emotional abuse—it is not a spiritual issue. The person and experience created the source of my pain. There are life experiences that impacted my beliefs about myself, causing me to question my value or feel I am "less than," and those experiences are not a spiritual issue. The spiritual issue is I am a creation of the Divine, worthy of love, respect, and dignity. The spiritual issue is I am good because the God Who created me is good. Dealing with the social and emotional issues helps me to disarm them of their impact in order to embrace the truth of God's word.

I am grateful the senior pastor sent me to therapy and didn't say "just pray about it." That is not to discount the power of prayer—I pray and meditate daily—but perhaps it was through my prayer and meditation that God led me to counseling.

If I broke my leg, everyone in church would look at me like I was crazy if I said I was just going to pray about it. If I broke my leg, they would say, "Go to a doctor." When something is hurting me emotionally that I can't heal, shouldn't it be okay to go to therapy? God uses that trained therapist to help me heal, just as he uses the medical doctor to set a broken leg.

Another aspect of the church view of therapy is this idea of being under spiritual attack. In my experience, attacks weren't spiritual; they were physical, verbal, emotional. People who attacked my self-worth by telling me I was stupid, a screwup, not good enough, and wouldn't amount to anything weren't attacking me spiritually; they were attempting to break my will to even try. Those who treated me like I wasn't good enough and shamed me for being poor weren't attacking me spiritually; they were draining me of hope and attempting to make me believe that I didn't deserve a better life. Those were emotional attacks, not what some would consider spiritual. Attacks on my self-worth and my dignity weren't spiritual warfare. They were negative social attacks that contradicted spiritual truths. Traditional old-school approaches to mental health do not serve us well now. Fortunately, I was in a church that did not perpetuate a stigma that mental health is a spiritual issue, that all I needed to do was pray.

As I still somewhat reluctantly began therapy for that fight with Mr. Breakfast, I was able to align prayer with the support of a professional who began to help me strengthen my emotional state and become more balanced. While God and I still talked regularly, I now had someone in the flesh to talk to, confidentially, who was trained to give me another perspective and tools to build my desired life.

CHAPTER 3

Haunted by the Past

My relationships with my therapists have allowed
me to become my authentic self on a sacred journey.
*Bishop Sharma Denise Lewis, Episcopal Area
UMC, Richmond, Virginia*

I remember the day I drove to see my therapist for the
first time. I was nervous. I didn't know what to expect.
I didn't know if he would be judgmental and view me
as some troubled broken person. When I arrived, I just
sat there in the parking lot for a moment trying to calm
down. I felt ashamed of myself and disappointed that I
had ended up in this situation—needing to see a therapist. I finally got out of the car and went into the office.
The therapist greeted me with a smile and a handshake,
then welcomed me in. It wasn't as bad as I thought. He
didn't seem judgmental at all. In fact, it just felt more

like a conversation rather than my assumptions it would be more of an interrogation.

Therapy opened a door for me to begin to go inside myself, to search out where my anger and dealings in situations like that with the homeless man were rooted. But I went to therapy and quit, meaning I started the process but didn't meet the challenge of being completely honest with a therapist. I showed up for the sessions, but in those uncomfortable moments, when we sat face-to-face and he looked into my eyes, it was almost as if he knew I was not telling the whole truth. The difficult first step for me was finding a level of comfort with the therapist. From the moment I began therapy, I knew deep inside that I needed it, even wanted it. I never reached a point when I actually quit, but at times I felt guilty about not being totally honest with my therapist. I realized he couldn't truly help me if I wasn't willing to tell the whole truth.

I think sometimes people quit not only because they are unable to tell someone else the truth, but because they are like me: At one time I wasn't even ready to admit the whole truth to myself. It is one thing to know the truth and wrestle with the hidden realities in your head, but it is so hard at times to speak the truth when that truth comes with so much pain and now you have to say it and name it. That is something I think people would just rather not do. I'd rather live with the pain instead of talking about it so that I can heal it. And a part of quitting is that we get to a point where we are so used to living with the pain that we don't even want to pursue peace or pursue being healthy. Sometimes healing hurts. A friend told me that when we attempt to find comfort with our pain, we are like a kid on a playground who gets a splinter, runs to his mom, and says, "Mom, I have a splinter and it hurts." But when she reaches to take it out, the child pulls back his hand and says, "No, if you take it out, it's going to hurt." In other words, sometimes we would rather stick with the pain we know than the pain we don't know, even if on the other side of that unknown pain is healing.

When I was a kid, I was playing football and broke my ankle. The doctor said it could heal without being reset, but I would always have a limp. If they reset my ankle—in other words, broke it again and aligned it—I would never have problems again. I would have balance and grow the way I was supposed to grow. As I struggled in those early therapy sessions, God brought that memory back to me. The experiences felt very similar. I was broken emotionally and I had to admit it. It was hard to admit. I would try to heal and move forward—or at least think I was healing—but what I considered progress was just suppressing or repressing a haunting memory. That is not healing. Blocking out the parts of my past that I wanted to forget ever happened, and not talking about them with my therapist, was the emotional equivalent to walking through life with a limp. The therapeutic process was like a re-breaking—living those haunting moments again! Letting the pain out and speaking it was excruciating, because in that moment of speaking it, I was feeling it again. Revisiting those experiences was one thing I didn't want to do, and I almost quit. I didn't want to feel that way again. I didn't want to be reminded. I just couldn't go back. In therapy, I had to break the bone again—go back to those haunted moments of my past. And I won't lie: It hurt! But that childhood football injury reminded me: We're breaking it again to realign everything so that when it heals this time, it heals the right way and I'll be able to grow and have balance.

God gave me a glimpse of what therapy offers, and God's spirit enabled in me a willingness to push past the pain, believing that on the other side of this pain are healing, alignment, and balance, and I'll never have to feel this pain again. I'll learn to detach my present emotional state from my past pain. I won't be haunted, shackled by these hidden stories. It's not that I won't remember them…I'll remember them from a different perspective. I'll be able to talk about the time when I was broken as someone who is now healed. I'll rejoice in my healing rather than be anxious that the past will recur or be fearful that something good will lead to or trigger pain. I will have learned to love myself. Since love is an inside job, I will have done the work.

That childhood football injury healed. I hardly remember which ankle was broken. I no longer feel the pain of that reset bone; the break is no longer there. Memories that once haunted me, hidden, shameful, are etched on my brain because they did happen, but by sticking with the sometimes painful process of therapy, I am now detached from what happened back then and I move forward, becoming more and more emotionally healthy. I feel good about myself, proud that I did the work to confront my past and heal, so that I no longer have to carry the weight of it.

That painful process began in a session when my therapist said, "Romal, you are never going to get your life right until you deal with the issues between you and your mom."

That made me angry. And I was there for anger management. "How are you going to bring my momma into this?" I challenged. "My momma ain't got nothing to do with me and this homeless man getting into it at church." When he said he was trying to help me, I thought I would call his bluff. "You think this is attached to an issue with my mom? Okay, cool, I'm calling my momma and I am bringing my mom up here."

So after the session with my therapist, I took his advice. I called my mom and said, "Mom, listen, I got in a fight at church."

"What are you doing getting in a fight at church?"

"Mom, it's a long story, I have to explain that later, but the pastor put me in anger management and my therapist says that I am never going to get my life right until I deal with the issues that you and I had during my childhood."

"We don't need no therapist all up in our business. We can fix our stuff ourselves."

"Mom, I know. If you come, these mandatory sessions can be over quicker."

"All right, fine. That therapist doesn't know what he is talking about, but if he thinks it is going to help you, I'll come up there."

After about four sessions or so, my therapist became even more direct with his thought on the cause of my anger. He told me that overcoming my anger was tied to dealing with the challenges of my childhood. My mom's addictions were a source of my anger; I was angry with her for choosing drugs over me, for leaving me with my grandparents. Even though I had overcome many of the external aspects of my past, inside I was still mad about all that went wrong. He said the time had come for me to stop living as a character trapped in an old family drama.

My mom and I were reluctant, but we went to therapy together. We had never talked about the ugly part of our life together. Like many families, we just tucked the pain away, never brought it up, and acted like it had never happened. We acted as if her past drug addiction, and how it shaped our lives, were not a part of our story, our truth. The ride to the therapist's office was awkwardly silent. Neither of us knew what to say to each other, so neither of us said much at all. I think my mom was stressed. She smoked several cigarettes in the car. We didn't say it to each other, but we knew that we were going to have to talk about things that for years we had been pretending never happened.

When we arrived, we went right in. He greeted my mother and invited us to sit down. It wasn't a couch session. We sat next to each other in chairs, and he positioned himself in another chair in front of us. The conversation started off light. He asked her about her flight, questions about the weather in California, then finally he asked if she knew why she was there. My mom said, "Romal asked me to come because of some issues he's been having, so I'm here to help my son." Just to hear her say, "I'm here to help my son," was a break-through for me. I'd never heard her say anything close to that before. I could already tell that I was probably going to cry during the session. I did—I cried throughout the session.

From the moment she stated why she was there, things moved rather quickly. That session was perhaps one of the most healing moments of my life. The therapist guided us through a conversation in which I felt safe enough to tell my mom about what happened during my childhood—things she was unaware of until that moment. I told her how as a child I felt afraid when she left me home alone, how it felt when I had to panhandle to get home from school because I had no money to get home, causing me to ask strangers for money. I told her about the times I had nothing to eat. I told her how humiliating it was to feel like a beggar; how sad and alone I felt when she was drunk, high, or passed out in her room; times I had no one to talk to. I told her about the day that I got jumped into a gang…we learned during my physical to enter the Army that it had fractured one of my ribs. That day after I got jumped, I was in pain. I came home and walked into her room. She was passed out, so I just went in my room, got into bed, and cried. I was hurting and she wasn't there for me. I told her how embarrassing it was that everyone knew she was a drug addict. I never wanted to hang out with gang members, but I needed help and no one else was there for me. I shared how people treated me badly because of her, the shame I felt and the anger I had been living with. I told her about unforgotten experiences that had made me sad and led to anger. A lot came up in that session.

Having a trained professional facilitate, or guide, the conversation between my mom and me was critical. I'm pretty sure that without the therapist, both of us would have been defensive and we would have argued. He helped us to listen to each other. Because of the guidance provided by the therapist, my mom was patient enough to hear me, listening with tears streaming down her cheeks. When I'd finished, she said what I had been waiting to hear for so long and didn't even know that I needed to hear it. My mom waited a few very long seconds for me to finish, making sure I'd gotten it all out, before saying the words that have been so healing to me: "Romal, I'm sorry. I never meant to hurt you."

That's what the hurt little boy within me needed to

hear: that she cared and that I mattered to her. Her apology meant so much to me. I needed to know that it wasn't her lack of love for me that prevented her from being there for me; it was her addiction. At that time of our session, she had been in recovery for several years. To hear her say "I'm sorry" was liberating. I became less and less angry over time.

Acknowledging my pain, owning her role in it, and simply saying "I am sorry" gave me permission to begin a new story that focused on the future rather than the past. This is what I mean by love is an inside job. In looking back at my past to heal the present, I examined experiences that made it difficult for me to love myself or anyone else. When I talk to people with family members who are addicts, I always tell them never to give up on that person. It took more than ten years for my mom to finally get help to overcome her addiction, but it happened. It's never too late, and as long as that person is still here, the story is not over. Healing can happen, not only for the person struggling with addiction, but also for the family members who have been living in pain because of it.

From the day my mom said she was sorry, our relationship began to flourish. Healing—the journey to self-love—had begun. By then my mom was off drugs, and after that session our relationship was better because we were no longer hiding anything. I wasn't hiding my pain. She was courageous enough to help me heal by apologizing and listening to me. For the remainder of her life, we had some amazing moments together. She was a good grandmother to my children. During the holidays, I would fly her up and she would buy all kinds of toys and spend time with them. I could see the joy it brought her.

Getting into a tussle at church was certainly not appropriate, but by the grace of God, that situation opened the door for me to begin the process of learning to accept God's love, to love myself despite my problematic past, and to love others. It was embarrassing to be sent to anger management and therapy, but it was what I needed. I was able to see the value of sitting down with a professional who knew how to listen the right way and then to guide me along the journey of finding my true self.

Some say you can't heal the past. True to an extent. You can't change what happened, but you can change how you understand what happened. You can change what you keep telling yourself *today* about what happened *yesterday*. No, you can't change what happened, but the way you *choose* to remember it and live its impact can be evidence that you are still in pain.

My mom and I no longer acted like our past didn't happen. I changed how I *thought* about what happened. We confronted the secrets and didn't have to pretend or evade anymore. The truth really did set us free. Harboring secrets is like holding your breath. They can suffocate you. When you are finally willing to exhale and let it out, you can breathe. My mom and I could finally breathe. I no longer lived a past-driven present.

The way I told myself the story of my childhood was based on who I was as a boy, who Mom was when she was drug addicted. But I was grown when we went to therapy. I learned that "Today is based on who I am now, not who I was then," and that slowly began to make sense. Being angry about the challenges I had as a child, and staying angry about them, was getting in my way as an adult. My anger was preventing me from living the life I wanted. Anger was not allowing me to be me. Allowing myself to be controlled by anger about what happened years ago had little to do with the present moment, and it was robbing me of the precious present.

I was rightfully angry about what happened then. It was unfair, it wasn't right, it shouldn't have happened. All of that is true. But I could choose to stop being angry now based on how I lived in the present moment. I didn't need to hold today accountable to what happened yesterday, because in the present moment I had the right to choose my path and even understand myself differently in light of what happened back then. I was angry then, but I am not angry now. Anger management worked!

I was hurt by my past. I was disappointed by those who shaped my childhood and youth. But in this present moment I have the opportunity to take ownership of my feelings and my life for today and also for tomorrow. I choose not to remain angry about what happened back then, because that anger causes me to disrupt my life now. I won't let that past pain prevent me from fulfilling my destiny and my divine purpose.

CHAPTER 4

Change Is a Contact Sport

For eighteen years, the support of therapists has helped me navigate challenging thoughts, feelings, and behaviors. This support enables me to create the life I truly desire. I have no idea who I would be or what type of life I would have without the help of trained mental health professionals. I am immensely indebted to the field.

Patricia Lesesne, elder, Presbyterian Church
(USA), Philadelphia, Pennsylvania

That therapist-guided, almost forced, confrontation with my mom helped me own how I felt and understand how my feelings about the past were having a harmful impact on my behavior, as in the situation with Mr. Breakfast. "This is the way I have always done things, so I need some help to change how I react to situations," I said to my therapist.

"Before you will be able to change your behavior," he replied, "you'll have to change your thinking. Thoughts guide behavior."

I guess therapy is not over, was my initial thought, bringing me down from the euphoria I'd felt from my mother's apology. I realized I had been conditioned to think the way I did, and I knew I couldn't change by myself. So I made the decision to continue therapy, voluntarily. I welcomed the help of someone who was impartial, and even though my therapist didn't fully know me, I'd learned that a trained therapist wanted the best for me. A therapist's job is to help people like me deal with trauma-inducing pasts and heal. And I now accepted that I was wounded.

When I decided to continue therapy by choice—and to pay for it with my own money—I saw it as a way of being able to open up to a professional who has the ability to listen to me, hear what I'm saying, filter out the challenges I'm having, and guide me to see what I'm not seeing about my own behavior. The therapist could give me the constant reminders I needed: that I am not my past, that I am constantly becoming, and in my becoming process, there is always opportunity to grow, heal, and do things differently.

Therapy was my chance to free myself to truly be who

I was meant to be. Through counseling sessions, I was guided to give voice to what I'd buried for so long. I felt a deep release. I no longer had to hide parts of my story. In speaking confidentially to my therapist, I was able to acknowledge the impact of those haunting experiences, admit how they hurt me, and own that hurt, not pretend it had no effect, not hiding or running from it. Through the therapeutic process, I was able to find a way to feel the pain for one last time and then move on. What I mean by that is this: When I used to think about some experiences, they would make me sad, angry, or afraid, so I would avoid thinking about them. I didn't want to think about the nights that I was so hungry I just wanted to go to sleep because I knew my mom was out drinking and was not coming home. Through counseling, I was able to confront those experiences and see them for what they are—past painful realities—and then detach my current emotional state from them. I could now look back at the experiences of trauma, verbal and physical abuse, and attempted sexual molestation and see what those experiences could do to me: take away my self-confidence, my desire to dream big dreams, my value. Those experiences had convinced me that I'm not worthy, that I'm not good enough, and that I am only here to be used and abused. Therapy enabled me to look back at those experiences and say, "It is not true. Those things happened but they don't have to continue to produce those feelings in me every time I think about them. I don't have to treat the memory of them like they are real now. When they happened back then, especially in my childhood, I did not have the ability to do anything about that. I was not in charge. When I was a kid, other people had the responsibility of nurturing me, protecting me, instilling value in me, speaking life to me, and inspiring me, and just because those things didn't happen sometimes, at critical times when I needed them, doesn't mean I am not worthy. I am worthy. Those people are accountable for their actions or failure to act. What they did or didn't do neither determines who I am nor dictates my future."

Therapy allowed me to take the power back from those past experiences that hurt me. I began the slow process of countering the many ways those experiences shaped me as an adult. I was enabled to take control of the narrative of my past and embrace what God says about me. In the words of the Psalmist: "I will praise you because I am fearfully and wonderfully made; your works are wonderful, I know that full well" (Psalm 139:14 NIV). I started to believe it to be true about myself.

To play the lead in my life and write a new narrative

was empowering. It was positive, hopeful, and based on the confidence that I am capable, that I am enough. It was not dependent on what anyone says or does. Trust in God and belief in myself were the roots of my courage. Outside support from others is confirmation of what I already know about who God is and who I am created to be. I'm grateful for the support of friends and family because it's the evidence that I am right about God and right about me.

My family, like just about every family, always had its challenges, but things got worse around 1984, when I was about fourteen. Up until that time, my mom and I, along with my uncles, aunt, and cousin, would visit my grandparents' house every other weekend. My grandmother would make dinner, everyone would sit around talking, and in the evening we would all go home. At times, arguments, even fights, took place during those gatherings, mostly when someone drank too much alcohol. It was rare, but sometimes the police had to be called. Oddly enough, these experiences did not seem that bad to me. I was used to it. They were normal. Typically everything worked out, all of us went home, and we would all return to my grandparents' home again in a week or two for dinner. Gathering as a family on those weekends was a bond that held us together.

Everything changed in 1984. That was the year crack cocaine seemed to flood my community. This may sound inappropriate, but it's the most apt metaphor I can think of to describe the devastation: Crack cocaine was my community's 9/11 and my family's burning, collapsing Towers. Our neighborhood was destroyed by addiction, street violence, prison, and the "war on drugs." I witnessed it up close. Addiction tore my family apart, and to this day we have not recovered. We stopped coming together for dinner at my grandparents'. Family members started stealing from each other (brothers and sister), even from my grandparents. Some relatives lost their jobs because they chose getting high over going to work.

My mom and I lost our apartment, and I ended sleeping on the floor at my grandparents' house. All of our belongings were stored in a shed in the backyard. When I was sad and wanted to be alone, the only place I could go was the hall closet in my grandparents' house. Sometimes I would fall asleep in there, dreaming and hoping life would change. The people I would sometimes turn to for help—my uncles and aunt—were no longer there for me, let alone for each other. Drugs and addiction became more important than our family bond. It became an "every man for himself" way of living. We've never been the same family since. The wounds caused by addiction have never healed among us. For most, the addictions didn't end. I was thrust into an emotional and social survival mode. I had to take care of myself as best I could. I felt abandoned. I was abandoned.

Drug abuse of all kinds continues to spread in the United States and abroad. Other communities are now being impacted. As a speaker, when I travel around the country and even abroad, I meet people from all races and backgrounds who share their stories of the pain their families are experiencing because of addiction. The actions of the addicted person and family members take a toll on their emotional health and create doubts about their life outcomes. I know. Addiction in my family made me cease to dream, feel uncertain about the love of God, and not love myself. I have found that God is all I have to hold on to; faith and hope are what give me the strength to keep going. I've heard it said, "You never know that God is all you need, until God is all you have." Learning to love God, love myself, and love others is at the core of healing.

Love is an inside job. It's the work of healing emotional wounds and becoming who you are truly meant to be. There are times when I hold the words God spoke to the prophet Jeremiah close to my heart: "'For I know the plans I have for you,' declares the LORD, 'plans to prosper you and not to harm you, plans to give you hope and a future.'" (Jeremiah 29:11 NIV). I whisper, "God, me too, do it for me too."

I revisited those haunting experiences from my childhood many times in therapy. It wasn't a once-and-for-all remedy. My therapist would ask me: "When was the first time you felt that way?" I would then have to sit and reflect and think back to the very first time I felt a certain anger, fear, or anxiety. For example, I have at times felt like my existence, my presence, doesn't matter in the world. When asked when was the first time I felt that way, I recalled a situation one night with my mom. I was around fourteen years old. I woke up in the middle of the night and went to the bathroom. I realized my mom's bedroom light was on, and as I walked to the bathroom, I saw her getting high. I hid in the bathroom and watched her make crack cocaine and then smoke. I was devastated. I knew she was on drugs, but that was the first time I saw her get high and watched the entire process. It was probably the most miserable moment in my life. When I snuck back into my room, I heard her say, "I hope you learned something, you stupid _____." (You can fill in the expletive.) I got in bed, stared at the ceiling, and with tears in my eyes, prayed, "God if this is what my life is going to be like, then I don't want to live." That was the first time I felt like my life, my existence, didn't matter. Therapy helped me confront and get honest about what that memory did to me, and then helped me no longer define my value by the pain of her words.

I slowly made connections between what happened then and what is happening now. I learned to disconnect the present moment from the past experiences. As I lived the present moments, I could experience them in a new way, where I took authority over my feelings. Gradually, I could both experience my feelings and evaluate them at the same time. I was no longer just *reacting* to challenging situations; more and more, I could choose a *response*—choosing to be empowered, not powerless. Slowly, I began to find a new way forward that is positive and that has value to my life now.

Sometimes during conversations, when people bring up the past and talk about what they cannot do because of their past experiences, what they shouldn't try, and what they're not good at, I'll ask questions I have been asked in therapy: What is the value in feeling that way about yourself? What good is believing that you can't do something, that you're not good enough, that you shouldn't try? These are questions I asked myself over and over. When I feel anxious, afraid, or am about to say I can't do something, I still ask them. I still have to silence my inner voice that tells me what I can't do, that I'm not worthy, or that great life experiences are not for me. When I hear, "This is not for people from where you come from or for kids who grew up poor," I've learned to have this inner dialogue: "What is the value of thinking that I'm not as deserving as anyone else? There is no value in that. The only reason I am choosing to believe that I am not good enough and that I shouldn't try is because I am holding on to a narrative that is no longer true for me. That this is not for me is based on past negative experiences or something someone else did, which led me to believe the current moment is not for me, but that is not true. I have the ability to do whatever I want to do with my life. Whatever dreams I have, I have a right to pursue them."

Like people who discouraged me from going to therapy, I sometimes fall back into the belief that I should just get over the past and move on. An inner voice says: "Oh, just get over it." I have to remind myself that getting over the past is an unrealistic expectation. Some things are far too complicated to just get over. Instead of admonishing myself to "just get over it," I need to admit to myself that I don't want to deal with it. I don't want to be reminded of the negative experience because I may feel guilty, sad, helpless, or ashamed. Believing I can just get over it is an attempt to deny what actually happened. Pushing my way through and persevering through haunted thoughts without examining them or refusing to let myself acknowledge their pain only suppresses my memories and feelings. I know that is not helpful. I must, through counseling, confront the memory and redeem what it took from me, heal that hurting place, and move forward without the baggage of the past. Then I won't have to run from it anymore. I don't have to hide or act like it doesn't exist. I can look at it head-on and say, "This is the last time I am going to feel this way about what happened and the last time I am going to let it haunt and torment me." I can be courageous and choose to fight for my emotional freedom and peace of mind. I will not run from the past because it doesn't go away; it has to be dealt with once and for all.

When I first went to therapy, I knew deep down inside that I was hiding parts of myself. Because I was hiding experiences that hurt me, I couldn't fully be me. I sensed I wasn't being totally honest with myself, and I knew I couldn't be honest with others. I felt like when people looked at my life from the outside, it looked good, but I didn't feel good. I felt like I was acting a part.

There was nothing that I could buy, attain, or do that was making that feeling go away.

Before I ever engaged in therapy, I had begun to realize that I had unsatisfying patterns of behavior and challenges with love, happiness, and peace of mind. I didn't understand how to get beyond that sense of frustration and love and enjoy my life. One girlfriend used to always tell me how proud she was of me whenever I accomplished something. Sometimes she said it out of the blue, when I hadn't done anything at all. I hated it. It irritated me. I felt she was being condescending and treating me like a child who needed to be told he's making someone proud. Now looking back, I realize I didn't appreciate my own accomplishments. I was never satisfied. I was always seeking something bigger to make me feel good about myself, and nothing I did was ever enough. I was like a drug addict chasing the euphoria of that first high because it felt so good. I was never going to do enough to soothe my internal pain and torment. I could not appreciate her being proud of me because, inside, I wasn't proud of myself. I didn't think I was good enough. No matter what I did, purchased, or achieved, the feeling I sought was never coming. Even when she said she loved me, it fell on deaf ears because I didn't love myself. I couldn't welcome those words from her.

I had so much to be grateful for, enjoy, and appreciate. I wanted deeper relationships, but I would self-sabotage those relationships. I wanted to be loved, but when people tried to love me, at a point I would push them away. I realized what I was doing, but I didn't know why or how to stop myself. When things went well and everything was clicking on all cylinders like being in the car and getting all green lights, life was good. Then I'd become anxious and afraid that it was going to be taken away, feeling like a crash was imminent. Once I got to counseling, I learned to ask: "Where is that coming from? My life is fine. Why do I keep feeling afraid that it is going to be taken from me?"

I was able to understand that life experiences from my childhood created my belief that good things would be taken from me. As a child, when I wanted to be loved, love had been taken from me. As a boy, when I finally found comfort in a home or in an apartment, we would eventually have to move. Everything was temporary as a kid. Now as an adult, I had that same fear that one day this, too, would be gone; someone was going to take it from me; life wasn't going to stay this good. Because of conversations with therapists, I am able to rationally understand that I was a kid then. I had no control over my living conditions. I had no ability to articulate my desire for love and affection from the people who were supposed to care for me. But as an adult, I have control over my circumstances and my living environment. I can communicate to people who love me—if I am courageous enough and let go of my pride—that I need to feel loved, I need you to affirm me.

THE LANGUAGE OF LOVE

One of the other things counseling helped me to understand was that it was hard for me to express love and communicate love for others in a way that they needed it. I was in another relationship at the time, and the love language of the woman I was dating—to borrow a concept from Gary Chapman's *The 5 Love Languages: The Secret to Love That Lasts*—consisted of words of affirmation. Every now and then she would ask me if I loved her and I would say yes. She would follow up with another question and ask me why. She may as well have asked me why water is wet. I had no clue, no answers as to why I loved her. I just did. I lacked the ability to express my feelings or articulate why I loved her. Trying to find the right words was like searching for water in the desert. I had nothing, and it left her feeling like my love was merely a mirage.

After counseling led me to finally reflect on my relationship with my mom, I came to believe that what I needed most growing up was love. I'm not talking about the practical kind of love, though I could have used more of that. I'm talking about emotional love, feeling a connection to another person who showed affection and affirmed my value just because I was me and worthy of it.

My grandfather was dying from asbestos poisoning the first time he told me he loved me and wasn't drunk. He worked at the shipyard, and after a long day, he would sit in the driveway at home drinking with his friends. When it got dark outside, Daddy, as I called him, and the guys would call it a night. He would come in the house and sit silently in his living room chair watching television. After a while, he would smile and call me over and, with boozed breath, give me a kiss on the cheek before saying, "I love you." I would hug him and go back to sitting next to my grandmother Jeanette, whom I called Momma. That's the only way I had ever heard my grandfather express his love until I was twenty years old and serving in the Army.

When I received notice that he was dying, I immediately flew back to California from Fort Stewart, Georgia. When I walked into his room, I couldn't help but notice how weak he looked, lying there, hooked up to an oxygen tank. Asbestos makes breathing difficult. I sat on the edge of the bed and gave him a hug. We looked at each other, with tears in our eyes. He became the first sober person in my family to tell me that he loved me.

My mom was a different story. Like my grandfather, she was an alcoholic, but much less functional. She would come home late at night, stumble into the bathroom, and kneel down to pay homage to the porcelain god (also known as the toilet), making her offering of regurgitated alcohol and uttering, "Oh my God, oh my God." When she was able to make her way to her room and climb into bed, she would call for me. "Romal, come here."

I'd walk into her room and stand at the side of the bed. "Yes, Momma."

"Listen," she'd say. "If I don't make it, I want you to know that I love you. You know I love you, right?"

"Yes, Mom," I'd reply, then kiss her on the cheek (while holding my breath) and give her a hug, thinking, *What you need to love is a breath mint.* Afterward I would go back to my room and go to sleep, grateful she made it home safely.

Much like my grandfather, my mom did not say she

loved me—while sober—until she was off drugs many years later. The first time was in the letter I received just after I'd graduated college and right before my first sermon, letting me know she was clean, sober, and attending church.

My grandmother "Momma," who I loved more than anyone or anything in the world, never said "I love you" during my childhood—although she didn't drink. It just wasn't something our family said—not my uncles, cousins, or aunt. Momma didn't tell me she loved me until I was twenty-three years old. By then I was in college and going to church because my girlfriend made me. One day I heard a sermon about love. The preacher talked about how people should confess their love for one another.

More than anything, I wanted to try this love thing out with my family members. Whenever I called home, my grandmother was the person I talked to the most. It would always make her smile to know that I was in college and hear how well I was doing. I decided to try this love thing out on her. This was new territory for me, so I was a little uncomfortable and nervous the first time. I didn't know what to expect when she responded. But getting my grandmother to say "I love you" wasn't as easy as I thought; it took about a month and went a little something like this:

End of Call 1
    Me: Mom, I love you.
Mom: All right now.

End of Call 2
    Me: Momma, I love you.
Mom: Okay, baby.

End of Call 3
    Me: Mom, I love you.
Mom: I know.

End of Call 4
    Me: Mom, I love you.
Mom: I love you too.

I did it! I could sense the smile on her face when she said it. It felt good to hear, and I believe it made her feel good to say it. Thinking back, I believe that was my first lesson about the power of real love. Love is persistent, resilient, determined, unwavering in its commitment. It wasn't just that I needed to hear her say "I love you"—I did—but she needed to verbally express her love. It meant a lot to both of us.

I was afraid to be affectionate, to fall in love or communicate love. If I love this person, I thought, one day they will walk away. I loved my mom and I knew my mom loved me, but when her addiction took her from me, it instilled in me a belief that people who love you, people you love, will choose something else. I learned from my childhood that I don't come first. Everyone except my grandparents seemed always to choose something else over spending time with me—sitting and talking with me. I believed I was never going to come first for anyone. No one would ever choose me and sacrifice for me. Rooted in that past experience, not in the present, I sabotaged relationships. I never gave people a chance because I operated out of these assumptions: This is temporary; they are not going to choose me first, so I'm not going to fully commit; I am not going to give them all of me because I need to emotionally be okay when they eventually walk away. I could never fully love. I could never fully trust because I treated everything as temporary.

The counseling process helped me begin to understand that love is commitment, trust, and longevity in relationships. The voices and the stories of my past don't haunt me anymore and make me afraid of love. I do not let myself be browbeaten by the past pain anymore. I've finally stood up to that bully and won. The past is like the wizard from *The Wizard of Oz*. When you finally see him behind the veil, he is a little guy who is not as tough as you thought. But he knew that as long as he kept you running, you'd think he was bigger than he actually is and you would not confront him. Those experiences of the past that hurt aren't as insurmountable as you think. When you confront them and see them for what they are, you discover how strong you are—and how amazing, gifted, talented, beautiful you've always been.

I can think about the past, revisit it, or even have someone bring up something from the past to me, and it doesn't change how I feel about myself. I learn from it now. I am strong enough now emotionally and psychologically to have conversations about what used to cause me pain and still maintain my joy and peace.

It is so liberating! The process of doing the inner work has helped me find my innovative self, see life as an amazing journey, and feel excited about the future, rather than afraid of it. I want to share what I know with others because all of us have a story, all of us have a past, regardless of culture, gender, social location or economic state, race, or any other defining factor. As humans, we all experience the same emotions. We have all been hurt and disappointed; we've all been let down. The emotional experiences of life are the same for all of us. Our confidence in the thing we believe we are good at is often shaped during childhood by the positive reinforcement received from parents and other family members. The same is true for our doubts. I didn't receive a great deal of positive feedback or reinforcement growing up, but I was told what I could not do pretty often.

SELF-DOUBT

For most of my life I've wrestled with self-doubt. When I was in high school, I wasn't a good student, because I had been convinced by the verbal abuse of family members that I wasn't smart enough. One of my uncles went to college to play football; it was cut short when he shot someone and then went to jail. No one I knew from my old neighborhood went to college. My mom did go to night school to further her education but still became a drug addict and alcoholic. The thought that college and a good education could change my life seemed like a stretch. I had a lot of doubts…mostly about myself based on what I had seen and experienced. I internalized all of it.

As an adult, I've still wrestled with self-doubt. One of my first jobs out of college was on Capitol Hill. I worked for one of my mentors, Doug Tanner. Doug always believed in me and even thought that one day I could run the organization, but I didn't think it was possible. It was hard for me to believe that lobbyists, members of Congress, and their chief of staff would embrace me as a leader. A part of my job as Deputy Director of Programs and Development was to organize events for members of Congress and other leaders to attend. These events would address issues such as poverty, education, or civility among members with different political party affiliations. More often than not, I felt out of place at the gatherings. I felt like everyone was smarter than me, came from a better family or community, and I believed they were just better than me. Even though I had two degrees from very good schools, I felt small when I attended gatherings or walked through the hollowed halls of Capitol Hill. I had convinced myself that even though I was there and had earned my right to be there, I was still on the outside looking in. I felt small because I chose to believe that I was small.

My self-defeating thoughts remind me now of a biblical story in which Moses sent a group of men to explore the land that God had promised to the people. When they returned with a report of what they saw, they said, "We saw the giants (the descendants of Anak came from the giants); and we were like grasshoppers in our own sight, and so we were in their sight" (Numbers 13:33 NKJV). In essence, just like these men, I had imposed a belief on myself that gave others permission to believe those same things about me. If you see yourself as small, you give others permission to see you as small. Self-worth does not depend on how other people see you but how you see yourself.

I'm not sure exactly when I came to the realization that I needed to do something about the self-defeating belief that fed into my self-doubt, but I know it was during therapy. Conversations with my therapist often seem to point to some form of inner work that I need to do in order to change my belief.

I don't think that I've solved or conquered self-doubt, but I think that I get up and try in spite of it. I'm not sure that everyone resolves his or her self-doubt. For some of us, we are able to cope with it better and confront our self-defeating thoughts when we sense they are rising up. I have listened to self-help coaches and some celebrities who claim to believe they can do anything. I believe I can do anything, but it has not eliminated the issue of self-doubt that inconveniently rises up within me. Sometimes there are opportunities where the bar is so high or the risk is so high that my tendency is to question whether or not what I want to accomplish can happen or I am good enough to make it happen.

The way that I now deal with these moments of insecurity is to ask myself a few centering questions: Why am I doubting myself? By asking that question, I am able to then provide an assessment of my reasons for thinking I can't do something or believing that I am not good enough. In asking the question, I then look at what is causing me to doubt myself. The next question is: What is it that I am choosing not to believe about my own capabilities? When I reflect on it, I am very much conscious of the fact that my doubt is not because I'm incapable, because I am certainly capable; it comes from the story I am choosing to believe about me—a story rooted in the verbal abuse of my childhood, which is not now nor was ever good for me and does not serve me well in the present moment. At times, those old memories play like a recording in my head and perhaps in my subconscious, leading me to believe the lie that I am not good enough.

I am able to overcome those thoughts, not by suppressing them but by taking the time to revisit the old stories from my past that created my doubts and realizing that what happened in the past is not my present reality. I then affirm that fact that I am capable because I choose to be capable. I am worthy because I choose to believe that I am worthy. I am able to overcome self-doubt by choosing to live into the present moment rather than holding on to a negative belief that would only hold me back. I affirm myself. I affirm the value that I choose to place on myself as an adult who is capable of making my own decisions rather than my inner wounded child, who felt powerless because of other people. I offer myself the love that I always wanted because love is an inside job with external implications.

Like you, I am who I was created to be. I am a person of value. I am a person who is worthy of love. I am a person who is capable. Sometimes I take a minute to meditate and center myself. I focus my awareness on God's presence. Rather than letting my thoughts be consumed by doubt, I choose to believe that God's spirit flows in and through me; therefore, I am capable and worthy because God is with me. So I trust God, and in trusting God, I trust myself.

Doubt will come, and when it does, I confront it, I question it, and then I dispel it with the truth of who I desire to be in the world and the person I desire to become. I then remove it and focus on where I am now, where I want to go, and who I want to be rather than giving too much attention to the doubt and what I could potentially be convincing myself that I can't do. There is no value in telling myself what I can't do, but there is significant value in believing in myself because at least, if nothing else, I will try.

I believe that moving forward in the presence of doubt is just like moving forward in the presence of fear. More often than not, fear and doubt go hand in hand. I think that doubt in many instances is rooted in fear or perhaps fear might create doubt, but when I confront it and I move in the direction of my desired life, I find that my level of courage and even my confidence increase because I was willing to be courageous enough to step out and try anyway. Someone has said that the only difference between a successful person and a person who deems themselves to be a failure is that the successful person steps out and tries even when they are afraid. The people who deem themselves a failure never even try because they are afraid. I don't know if I got that right, but I think what I am trying to say is, there are times when all of us have fears and doubts, and what separates us, what allows us to rise above the fray or to set ourselves apart, is to be that person, that man or that woman, who does it in spite of the fear, in spite of the doubt, and gives it a shot anyway. This is the only way you are going to experience victory. The only way you will ever live into your desired path and your desired outcome and the life you want for yourself is simply to step out and try even in the presence of doubts and fear and anxieties.

If you are carrying the weight of the past, unable to become who you are truly meant to be because of self-doubt, anxiety, fears, and worries, you are a lot like I was before I started seeing a therapist. Take the opportunity to tap into your stories and those experiences, and you can find the same healing that I've found. Telling my story in this book is an invitation for you to give voice to your own story. It is your permission to stop running, be courageous, and own your truth. Confront that bully; stand up to that haunting past and say, "Enough! I'm done. What happened is not going to keep shaming me and getting in the way of the life I want to live, the way I want to feel about myself."

If you don't want to just pretend to be happy or just talk about joy, if you want to genuinely know what joy feels like, say as I did: "I am going to confront anything that stands in the way, even if what is standing in the way is me."

CHAPTER 5

Who's Looking for Me?

I never wanted to see a therapist. I told myself, "Therapists are for really messed-up people and I'm, well, just struggling." I went to a counselor that first time and found it helpful. I kept going back week after week, and over several years I found something incredible was happening: I was being set free from invisible tethers that had held me captive for decades. With the help of a trained professional, I was able to better understand my own story and separate the truth from the fiction of my life and even my faith.

Wes Olds, campus pastor, Grace Church,
Cape Coral, Florida

I was twenty-four years old when I finally went to church. That was a big deal. I'm an introvert, but I had a girlfriend who went to church. It is a very big deal for an introvert to actually say in public, "I have a girl-friend," and then go to church when said girlfriend told me: "Look, I go to church. If you want to be with me, you've got to go to church."

"Hey, whatever it takes," I said. "Praise the Lord!"

As I began to embrace changes in myself and in relationships—like saying and hearing "I love you" from my grandmother—I would get to church Sunday morn-ings, hear the choir singing, and say to God, "Lord, this is so different from my life growing up. I don't know why You've given me the opportunity to be around such committed people. They really love You." I'd remember where I came from; we didn't do things like this: Get up at 6:15, 6:30, 6:45 in the morning on the weekend! Show up at the 8:00 service. I came from an environ-ment where we stayed out all night and slept during the day. I still live my life in the double digits—10:00 a.m. and later. (The safest time to walk through a dangerous neighborhood is in the morning because gangsters don't tend to be morning people; they were out all night do-ing what gangsters do.)

Being with people in the house of the Lord was in-deed a blessing and definitely different. In the moments when the ghosts of my past haunted me, my thoughts were silenced by the sounds of praise and worship. I could be at peace, even if for a moment. The people in church with their hands lifted in praise were a sign of hope.

I used to wonder what goes on in church. When I got to church, I found out: People in church loved to eat all the time; they were cooking and bringing great food; they always had events going on and would just hang. Sometimes the custodian had to threaten to turn the lights off in order to get people to go home. Did I mention the food? Church people love feeding you! They even like it when you ask for more. It was pretty awesome. I've always been skinny. More than fifteen years ago when I first started ministry, I would walk into a church where I was to be the guest preacher and tell the older church mothers that I was a preacher. Oftentimes, they would reply, "You don't look like a preacher," and proceed to bring me a big plate of food. In church, they will help you through things in life. I'd find myself reflecting on my childhood again, the times when my friends and I were hungry, when I was afraid or just felt alone, and I thought, I wish the people in church would have come outside and told us, done something to touch the lives of people like me, who didn't have someone to bring us inside. If I knew what was going on in there,

I would have come long before now. I wish someone would have just come outside and told us.

So I became a Christian while in college. I started sensing God speaking to me through the stories told during sermons. I learned to pray. The names "God" and "Jesus" took on meaning to me. I became a worshipper. I grew to worship God, not so much for what God did but because of Who the Almighty is. Attending Bible study and reading Scripture taught me that God is a god of love, a god of peace, a god of healing, a god of redemption, a god of restoration, a god of hope, a god of grace, a god of mercy, a god of every good and perfect gift—the source of strength, hope, dreams, goals, aspirations. I gathered with members of the church because of God, because I loved God and felt God's love for me. When I couldn't reach one of my goals and I was on the verge of giving up, God would somehow open a door of opportunity and renew my hope that things would get better. God blessed me in spite of myself and my past, saw the good in me, and I felt grateful and keenly aware of the presence of the Holy Spirit. It was in God, as I experienced faith in those early church days, that I began to live, move, and have my being.

About four years ago I was going through one of my

moody spells, feeling like I wasn't good enough. I prayed and asked God to show me if there were any people like me in the Bible. I stumbled across the story of Jephthah in Judges 11:1–11, 32. I had never read it or heard anyone preach or talk about it. Jephthah's story stuck with me. It's one I often tell to young people when I'm out speaking to let them know that just because you don't fit in doesn't mean you can't be great. Jephthah had some serious issues but, hey, so did the biblical leader David and preachers always seem to cut him a break.

I related to Jephthah:

He was a mighty warrior; his father was Gilead and his mother was a prostitute. Gilead's wife also bore him sons, and when they were grown up, they threw Jephthah away. You're not going to get any inheritance in our family, they said, because you are the son of another woman. So Jephthah fled from his brothers and settled in a land where a gang of scoundrels gathered around him and followed him. Later when the elders of Gilead were at war, they sought out Jephthah and said, "Come, be our commander so we can fight." Jephthah replied, "Didn't you hate me and drive me from my father's house?

Why do you come to me now when you are in trouble?" Then the elders of Gilead said to him, "Nevertheless we are turning to you now. Come with us to fight and you will be head of all of us who live in Gilead." Jephthah answered, "Suppose you take me back to fight the Ammonites and the LORD gives them to me, will I really be your head?" The elders of Gilead replied, "The LORD is our witness we will certainly do as you say."

So Jephthah went with the elders of Gilead and the people made him head and commander over them and then Jephthah went over to fight and the LORD gave them into his hands.

Judges 11:1–11, 32 NIV

For years I used to tell people that was my favorite passage of Scripture. But it is not. My favorite passage of Scripture is in Jeremiah: "'For I know the plans I have for you,' declares the LORD, 'plans to prosper you and not to harm you, plans to give you hope and a future'" (Jeremiah 29:11 NIV).

I held on to the Judges 11 text because it reminded me of my own life, being rejected for circumstances I didn't create. I resonated with biblical families who had challenges, who struggled, where everything wasn't perfect. This Scripture is about a young man who was pretty much thrown away. Just like Jephthah, I grew up in an environment where my dad wasn't there. He never married my mother. It was just me and my mom. That was all I had. My grandparents lived in another city. We lived in the projects, didn't have any money; my mother was a drug addict and my daddy wasn't there, and for these reasons some in the neighborhood and even in my family decided that I didn't deserve anything. They might as well have said: "Look at where you come from. Look at how you dress. Your family doesn't have an education. You live in the projects. You are not worthy. You don't deserve anything."

When I read that Jephthah fled to the wilderness, I could relate to that. When my mom and I lost everything, when all of our belongings were stored in a shed in my grandparents' backyard because she lost her job and we got evicted, my mother would go missing for months at a time and I found my place on the streets. The text in the New International Version says: "He fled to the wilderness where a gang of scoundrels gathered around him and followed him." Other versions of the Bible say "worthless men," and I felt that is how some thought of me. When they looked at me and other young brothers and sisters on the streets, their eyes said: scoundrels; worthless; look at where you've ended up; look at the families you come from. In church, those who were honest admitted they were the very families from which those young people come. Some even walked up to the altar to pray for somebody that others considered a worthless scoundrel, that they will seek God, believe that God will turn their lives around, that the best is still yet to come in spite of how they are living right now. The text says that Jephthah fled to the wilderness. The wilderness today is our streets. It's very much the same thing, and just as dangerous. I had to learn how to survive on the streets, to hustle. I hung out with gang members and from time to time sold drugs in order to buy school clothes and food.

The church that I attended when I first became a Christian also hosted a Boy Scout troop. I've learned that it's pretty common for churches to have Boy and Girl Scouts. Some kids in my neighborhood participated in the Scouts, but instead, most of us were recruited to sell drugs or join gangs.

I got an award several years ago from a national social justice organization in D.C. It seems like people love honoring young black men who come from the projects.

If you make it out, you will probably get a plaque. They will invite you to the stage to talk about how difficult it was to come from where you come from. We just want to honor you, they'll say. I called a cousin I grew up with and I said, "I am getting an award today."

She asked, "For what?"

I told her it was for people who used to be poor, come from the projects, and have done something a little different with their lives.

"We weren't poor!" she corrected me.

I said: "Do you remember Meals on Wheels? They used to come in our neighborhood and that was how we had dinner some nights."

"Oh yeah," she said.

"You remember how people didn't want to come in our neighborhood because of the violence and the drugs and crime? You remember how we couldn't pay our rent and how I went to different schools every year because my mom and I would have to move when we couldn't pay the rent?" We were poor; that was us. But my cousin was right, we didn't call ourselves poor. I didn't learn that we were poor until I had graduated from college, started working on Capitol Hill, and realized that people there placed labels on us: poverty, low income, working poor, welfare recipients. We didn't talk about ourselves that way. You had to be homeless to be called poor, unable to buy anything. We had a little something, even if we had to take things. But we weren't poor.

Jephthah learned to survive when he was in the wilderness. Scripture said a group of scoundrels and worthless men gathered around and followed him. I noticed that he was not by himself in the wilderness. Others were already there, and just like Jephthah, they had been thrown away. Somehow they made him a leader. When he showed up, they could see something in him that was different from everyone else, something that made them understand that this young man was a leader, that he had purpose. They gathered around him and followed him, not the people who should have seen something in him.

When I was on the streets, I hung out with what some would call "the wrong crowd" because I was in the wilderness. But when it felt like everyone else had thrown me away, they were the only crowd that I had left. No one else wanted us. I was a latchkey kid. I would get home after school and I'd play basketball and I'd stay outside because I didn't want to sit in the house. Being alone in the house left me with nothing but my thoughts. I wondered if my mother was coming home, if she would be drunk, if some man would bring her home and take advantage of her. I even wondered if I was going to eat that evening. Going outside was a welcome distraction. Some guys would come around and play basketball with me. They would play pickup. We selected teams and afterward they would ask me if I was thirsty. They would take me to the corner store and we'd get a gallon of sweet tea; they would get me some food and they just let me hang out. As the day drew on, they'd ask, "You want to come hang out? We're going to the park." They had a place near the park, a room they had broken into in one of the projects. It was set up real nice—a TV and a stereo, graffiti murals on the wall. They had put a lot of thought into the layout, as if it were their home. We weren't supposed to be down there, but that was our space. They never asked me to join anything; they just let me hang out. They treated me well. We had a lot in common. All of us had been thrown away. We had been rejected and labeled. I was told that I was stupid so many times by my mom because of her addictions, and told that I was not going to amount to anything. And the funny thing was, when I got bad grades, my mother, uncles, and teachers got mad at me. Wait a minute, I thought, you have called me dumb and stupid and said I wasn't going to amount to anything, and now I have proven you right and you're mad. (You never get positive outcomes from negative feedback, ever. It doesn't work.)

Hanging out with the homies (friends) one day, I asked, "Can I be down?" They treated me like I was one of them, but sometimes they would leave me out of certain gatherings. Certain places I wasn't allowed to go. When I asked them how I could be down, they said, it meant getting jumped in. I wanted to be with them. That was my family. That was all I had. My uncles lived across town; I couldn't commute all the time. I didn't have bus fare. These were my friends. The day came and I got jumped in, which meant I had to fight. Normally the process is one against three people, but I was small so an exception was made and I had to fight one of the older guys. He beat me like I stole something! Afterward I went home and cried myself to sleep. My mother was home, high and in her bed asleep; she never knew what happened.

In church, I first heard the story of Rahab—we still keep calling that woman a prostitute, when actually she was a courageous woman who understood what God was doing. And she did not just save herself. She had a hustler spirit. She cut a deal to save her whole family. She was just like my mom. I found reconciliation and redemption in her story, and it gave me hope. Everyone called my mom a drug addict, forgetting all of the things she had done before her addiction. After having me at the age of seventeen, she went back to school and got her diploma. She continued to stay focused and took classes at night to become a bank teller. Over time my mom climbed the ranks working in different banks until she finally landed at the Federal Reserve in Downtown San Francisco. But it seemed like everyone forgot all of that and saw her only as an addict.

Going to church reminded me of times when we would sit out on the street in an area we called the battle-field. A church sat across from the battlefield. Walking home from school, you had to make it across the battle-field, and if you got stopped, you had to fight to get home. Every Sunday that church over there would be packed. Folks dressed nice. Everything looked nice. I remembered the sunny days I would sit on the other side of the battlefield and watch people go into that church. I saw people going into the church and then the doors would close behind them. I always wondered what was going on in there.

A lady in our neighborhood who lived across the street from my grandparents would dress up her kids, and when they were all seated in her shiny car, she'd look over the hood at us sitting on the curb. She looked disgusted, as if to say how dare you all not go to church. But not once did she invite us to go with her.

As someone who was on the outside of church looking in, working hard to be like the people who didn't want me, I understand the church has to admit that we throw some people away. We look down on those who are not educated or because of the way they dress, what their families have done, and where they come from. Even without our words, the look on our faces says you don't belong around here. Look at you. You are not like us. We treat them like they don't belong in the house of the Lord, as if we get to pick who gets to be loved by God. God loves everyone, but in church we decide who gets to be loved around here. That arrogant Christianity kept me from church for the first half of my life. Often the very people who are thrown away are the ones God will use to redeem and liberate our communities because they know what is going on. Game recognizes game on the streets.

It has been said, you can lead a horse to water but you can't make him drink. My grandfather told me whoever said that never lived on a farm, because everyone on a farm knows that if you just put a little salt in the oats, it will make the horse thirsty. If we are truly salt and light to the world, we love people. If we love them, they'll come asking, "What must I do to be saved?"

When people like me are just off the streets, when we initially get to church, we don't know the rules. We don't know the songs or how church works. So I got to church because of my girlfriend, and the next thing you know, I end up becoming a Christian. Several years later after graduating from Divinity School at Duke University, I was asked to join the staff of a church—a little bit like Jephthah. I was told: "We want you to be on staff." Me: "What do you want me to do?" They said, "You're 'urban' so we want you to do urban ministry." Me: "Okay, cool. I'll go outside and be urban." After the incident with Mr. Breakfast, they began to call me Reverend Mike Tyson. There's a saying, "Everybody wants to be a beast until it's time to do what beasts do." The church wanted me to do urban ministry, but they were not ready for me to deal with situations the way things sometimes get dealt with in an urban context. I had a confrontation with Mr. Breakfast and anger management followed. But here's the backstory: I was responsible for the homeless ministry, community outreach, and pastoral care. We would bring the homeless to the church every Sunday, and they would eat with the congregants in the church cafeteria, also known as the fellowship hall. Eventually the church members didn't want the homeless eating with them at church and called a meeting to ask us to just pack up food for the homeless and let them sit together in the balcony. The homeless ministry, which I worked with, blocked that. The homeless remained welcome in the cafeteria with church members for a while until the power of church politics kicked in and they decided to stop serving breakfast altogether due to "budget concerns."

I accepted my call to ministry about four years before the Mr. Breakfast incident. Just weeks before my first sermon, I got a letter in the mail, a thick envelope from my mom. I was afraid to open it because, judging from the size of the envelope, it seemed like she had a lot to say. I thought, *This is some type of ghetto dissertation.* Typically when I got a letter or a call, it was nothing but bad news: Somebody either was in jail, needed bail money, or was killed. My uncle once asked me to send him twenty dollars via Western Union; he was in San Francisco, I was in Washington, D.C., literally on the other side of the country. It was going to cost me ten dollars to send him twenty dollars by way of Western Union!

I got a letter and it was thick, probably full of foolishness. I'm scared. *I can't open this*, I'm thinking. I've got to keep my mind right because I'm about to do my first sermon in a few weeks. If I was going to read the letter, I decided I would need some support. I called a few close friends in to meet me at church. My boy Larry sat with me and he read the letter. There I was, sitting on the front pew of the church in front of the altar on a Friday afternoon waiting on the verdict while Larry read the letter. I felt like I was sitting in a doctor's office waiting on a diagnosis that comes: "I'm sorry, Romal, but the results came back positive and you are ghetto. You are likely to experience hood tendencies including poor enunciation skills when you speak, playing inappropriately loud music while driving, and putting unnecessarily large tires on your car. You'll likely learn to do a backflip before you can read. Although there is no cure for ghetto, we can help you control the symptoms—you'll need to go to therapy."

But in reality, Larry says, "Man, you need to read this."

My mom had never written to me before. The letter wasn't typed; it was handwritten on plain white paper. I always thought her handwriting was beautiful. She probably could have become an author if things had turned out differently. Line after line she showered me with praise for my accomplishments—the honors I received while in the Army, graduating at the top of my class from Howard University, becoming a Christian. She told me that she had her own apartment. All of it was a surprise to me. Not what I was expecting at all. *Romal, I heard you're about to be a preacher.* That was a big deal in my family. That was not what they were looking for; they thought I was going to be an athlete, play basketball, or run track, something to get them out of the projects. My family was full of contradictions. One minute I'm expected to be the ghetto superstar, but most days I was stupid. My uncle Roy used to say, "Tune is going to be the one to get us out of the projects. He's the one." Uh, not so much! When my family heard I was becoming a preacher, their reaction was, "Oh, we're stuck." Mom wrote, *I hear you're about to be a preacher and I want you to know I'm proud of you. I'm proud of you, son. I want you to know that I've always loved you. You need to know that I've been clean and off drugs for nine months now through a church. Amen, Amen. Through a church rehabilitation program. I've included with this letter my Bible study* (That's why it was so thick!), *and I was wondering if maybe one day you would call me and we could study the word of God together.*

A few years had passed since I received the letter from my mom. Since that time, I had gone on to graduate from Duke, work on Capitol Hill, and then left that job to go on staff at a church. It wasn't long before I had to make that awkward call—"Mom, I got in a fight at church." God was already preparing us both for effective counseling. She was off drugs and I was open to the idea of dealing with our past. God works through therapy. The altar and counseling office work together. God uses both. Every time you make your way to that altar and ask God for redemption for someone you love, just wait and anticipate what God will do in God's timing. In the meantime, do your own work.

God redeems. Kids, brothers, sisters, members of our extended families, and our communities need us. If God is going to redeem them, God is going to use you. We must both pray and show up in counseling in order to be there for them. We cannot give up on them. God is not done.

Come fight for us, Jephthah. Be the restorer of our community.

I am that same kid who panhandled for money to get home from school on the city bus. Me, the guy who was a hustler and went to a different school every year, whose momma was a drug addict. It's still me; it's still in me. It is a part of my story. But when the spirit of the Lord moved, and I was willing to step up and do my part, this same kid became an honor graduate, magna cum laude, all-American collegiate scholar, Who's Who in American Colleges and Universities from Howard University and Duke University. Because of who God is, because of people like Larry Sampson, Dean Dorothy Powell of the Howard University School of Nursing, and Mrs. Gail Cash, I'm still here and I'm not who I used to be.

When I was trying to change my life and didn't have a place to live, my friend Larry allowed me to stay with him and sleep on the couch. That friendship opened the door for me to find my love for ministry. Since I wasn't paying rent, his main requirement was that I had to go out with the homeless ministry to pass out sandwiches and drinks. At the time, Larry was in charge of the program. Years later in my role as clergy, that ministry became one I was responsible for as church staff.

During my junior year of college, my grandmother had a slight stroke and I wanted to drop out of school to go home and be with her. When I told my dean, Dr. Powell, she was determined not to let me go, fearing I would never come back and finish. Dr. Powell called my grandmother and encouraged her to convince me to stay in school. I did. Thank God, Dr. Powell was probably right: If I had gone home, it's unlikely I would ever have returned to Howard University.

Mrs. Cash was my saving grace on more occasions than I can remember. She worked for the School of Nursing and handled the emergency loan fund. This was a pool of resources the school would give to students when we were in serious need. I was always in serious need. I used to hang out in Mrs. Cash's office just to talk because she genuinely cared. Over time she knew my story and a lot about my family. Mrs. Cash would always encourage me to do well. She helped me believe in myself. In a sense, she was like family during a time when I missed my grandmother and was far from home.

During my time in the Army, numerous soldiers—male and female—encouraged me, even though I had a bad attitude. They were older, had seen a lot, and outranked me in both wisdom and leadership. I was accepted into Howard University right around the time the Kuwait war, Desert Storm, ended. The Army was downsizing and offering soldiers the opportunity to end our enlistments with full benefits providing we had completed at least three years of a four-year enlistment. I qualified but I missed the deadline to apply because I was out of town on leave. I thought I was not going to be able to get out of the Army in time to start school. School was to begin in August, but my full four-year enlistment would not be complete until November. I was discouraged. I told some of the older soldiers about it, and they jumped into action. Several of the women started doing the research to find out if there was a legal loophole that would allow me to get out in time to start school in August. They found one. There was a rule that said if a soldier had completed at least three years of a four-year enlistment and had proof of being accepted into college, then that person was eligible to receive full GI Bill benefits and be released from duty to start school. Without the help of those men and women in the Army who encouraged me, told me that I was smart, and still helped me—oftentimes in spite of myself—I may very well had given up on pursuing college. I owe them a great debt of gratitude.

Throughout my life, people have inspired me to keep going and set examples that I wanted to follow as a person, a leader, and a public speaker. My grandparents always believed in me, but the first person to tell me that I was smart was my tenth-grade math teacher at Hogan High School. One day when I was being disruptive in class, he walked over to my desk and just hovered over me, staring. After a long awkward silence, he reached out to shake my hand. While staring me in the eyes and on the verge of breaking my hand he said, "I'm going to need you to be quiet in my class. Do you think you can do that?" "Yes," I replied, and then he let go. A few days after that awkward moment, he asked me to stop by his house after school. When I arrived, he was out front cutting grass. He stopped when he saw me approaching and we sat on the porch. He asked me what I wanted to do with my life, and I told him I didn't know. And then he said, "Romal, you're smart. If you get your act together, you could really do something with your life and become somebody." No one had ever said anything like that to me before. I continued to be a class clown and rarely studied, but his words stuck with me.

After graduating high school as a barely passing student, I realized I had very few options. I never took the SAT and had walked out on the PSAT five minutes after admitting to myself that I knew nothing. I joined the Army. Basic Training was the second time in my life that a stranger ever called me smart. I always received high marks for physical fitness and basic performance skills, but just as in high school, I had a bad attitude. At the end of our eight weeks in Basic Training, each platoon had to choose their highest performing soldier. Four platoons were each divided by the type of job we would enter after training. My platoon, Fourth Platoon, or Hard Core Four as our drill sergeant called us, chose me to represent them in the competition to become soldier of the cycle. I had the highest scores over all in aptitude, marksmanship, and physical fitness. Each of the remaining platoons chose their representatives and then we had to compete by taking a test and performing military drills. Our scores were compiled at the end of the competition and I won. I became soldier of the cycle and had to deliver a speech on graduation day. After delivering the speech and closing out the ceremony, I was hanging outside with my friends. One of the drill sergeants walked up and said, "Tune, you're smart as hell but you have absolutely no military bearing." I didn't know what military bearing was, but what stuck with me was that for the second time in my life, someone who didn't know me called me smart. Over time, I started to believe it.

My high school girlfriend Toi taught me about historically black colleges and universities. While I was in the Army, we kept in touch. She told me that she was going to Howard University. I had never heard of the school. She said, "It's a black college, Romal." "You're lying," I said. "Just tell me the truth because there is no such thing as a black college." But she insisted: "They even have black professors." I said, "Sure. And I bet the school mascot is a unicorn, since we're making things up." "No, it's actually a bison," she replied. This was before Google and I didn't know what a bison was, so I just let her have the last word in that conversation. When she invited me to visit her during Howard's homecoming, my friend Courtland and I drove up from Fort Stewart, Georgia, together. He was familiar with HBCUs and was excited to go for the fun.

That trip to Howard changed my life. I had a blast drinking and hanging out with African American college kids. I never saw myself as someone in college. Even when I lived with my father in suburban Jersey, I always believed kids in college were smarter than me and came from better neighborhoods. One night while watching two guys mix drinks in a garbage can, I experienced a lightbulb moment that would begin my journey toward becoming an honor graduate. The guys mixing the drinks could not figure out the appropriate proportions of alcohol to fruit punch. I said to myself, "Oh my God, I can go to college! These kids are not smarter than me. I know how to make better drinks. They're not better than me; they've just had better life choices."

After homecoming, Courtland and I made the drive back from D.C., and on Monday morning I enrolled in night school. A year and a half later I was accepted to Howard University. After four years at Howard, I became the first person in my family to graduate—and with honors.

Looking back, it's clear that I have never been as alone in the world as I thought I was. God has always been looking out for me. God has used men and women from different walks of life to teach me what I didn't know and open doors of opportunity that I couldn't open for myself. When I was down and God wanted to encourage me, He used the voices of men and women to inspire me. When I needed to know that I was loved, God used the arms of compassionate people to console me. When I felt like God was distant from me, God used men and women of faith like Richard Rohr, Ned and Barbara Simmons, and Dr. Elizabeth Conde-Frazier to teach me prayer and meditation to draw close to God. And God used the church.

I first learned about tailor-made suits and French cuff shirts while attending church. My pastor at the time was an excellent dresser. I, on the other hand, dressed like an NBA draft pick in cheap polyester-blend suits that were clearly too big and "pleather" (fake leather) shoes. I watched my pastor from a distance and then mimicked his attire, as well as that of other well-dressed men in the church.

The church is also where I honed my skills as a

speaker. I listened to the rhythms and cadences. I watched the hand gestures, posture, even breathing patterns of speakers like Dr. Frederick Douglass Haynes, Bishop Vashti McKenzie, and Dr. Otis Moss III. I valued preachers and speakers who spoke from a variety of contexts, who had honed their craft and could tell great stories. Two of my other favorite speakers are Bob Goff and Michael Frost. Listening and watching carefully, I learned that what makes each of them great is simply being themselves and that I needed to learn how to find my own authentic voice and just be me.

Justice work in the church is where I first got involved in politics. Doug Tanner, founder of the Faith and Politics Institute, gave me a job as an intern while I was still a student at Duke University. Doug introduced me to Ronnie Moore, a political operative in North Carolina. I never knew exactly what Ronnie did, but he told me, "If you really want to know anything about politics, you need to work on a campaign." Ronnie made a call to the North Carolina Democratic Party headquarters in Raleigh, and I became the first Faith Community organizer they ever hired. I worked with and mobilized churches across the state. After I worked on the elections and graduated from the Duke School of Divinity, Doug hired me at the Faith and Politics Institute as Deputy

Director for Programs and Development. Doug, and so many others too numerous to name, have always seen more in me than I have been able to see in myself. I am grateful for the people who have played key roles in my life, whether they knew it or not, people I've watched and admired from a distance or who have taken me under their wing because, for some reason, they believed in me. They are my evidence that God has always been looking for me, that God has always had an assignment that was mine to complete. And I myself have always been an assignment.

God is looking for all of us.

Two years ago I was asked to lead a session at a conference hosted by a friend in New York. There was nothing atypical about the gathering. I stayed in the host hotel, where most of the conference attendees and speakers were staying. On the last day of the gathering, I was heading back to the hotel when I ran into one of my mentors, Rudy Rasmus, and his wife, Juanita. They're like family to me; I refer to them as my "uncle and aunt by choice." Rudy and I talk almost weekly, and I often ask Juanita to pray for me. She has an amazing gift for helping others heal emotionally and spiritually and is so tuned in to the Presence or Spirit of God that she can discern when something is not right with a person emotional or spiritually. It freaks me out sometimes that she knows when something is wrong, even if I don't tell her. She's right every time. When I ran into Rudy and Juanita in the lobby of the hotel, Rudy greeted me with his typical uncomfortable twenty-second hug. (He's what I call an over-hugger.) Immediately after Rudy released me from his forever hug, Juanita asked, "Can I pray for you?" She didn't even say hello. Immediately, I knew this lobby interaction was going to be deeper and more spiritual than the typical greeting: hello/life is good/great seeing you/good-bye. Rudy knew it, too, and he casually walked away to let Juanita do what she does—pray. And so she prayed. There in the lobby, in full view of anyone who walked by, she held my hands and began to pray.

I don't know how long we were standing there. I can't remember everything she said. But by the end of her prayer, I was crying—the kind of cry where you need a tissue to blow your nose. The ugly cry.

The one thing I remember she said during her prayer was, "God says He had to take you this way." Her words were shocking and for a moment made me angry. Why would God take me through all the pain I've been through? It seemed unfair. I didn't understand her words at that moment. But I do now. God didn't *cause* any of my pain. Flawed and broken people did. In fact, some of it I caused myself. God brought me *through* all of it to where I am now. Juanita was right. God took me this way because I had to learn from my mistakes, learn to forgive, heal. And then somehow God had to show me how to be courageous enough to offer my story with all of my wounds and scars, messes and miracles, back to the world so that others might find the courage to stop sacrificing true happiness on the altar of public perception and know that redemption is possible.

God continues to look for me, the real me, the me that God created in God's own image. The more I confront the ghosts that haunt me and heal the life-limiting stories I have been telling myself, the more I am able to see myself the way God sees me. I have a deeper sense of knowing myself and knowing God. When I let God find me, the me that is good and fine just the way that I am, I draw closer to God and more deeply understand myself as a child of the Divine.

CHAPTER 6

Church Hurt

I pursued therapy after realizing that the contemporary church had no language to help me cope through what my grandmother would have called a "nervous breakdown." My psychiatrist named my condition a major depressive episode, and naming it then helped me discover that the early church fathers and mothers had a name for my experience: "dark night of the Soul." It's been a rich journey toward my recovery and I value the treasure that therapy helped me mine from the darkness.

Juanita Rasmus, pastor and spiritual director,
St. John's Church, Houston, Texas

They triumphed over him by the blood of the Lamb and by the word of their testimony.

Revelation 12:11 NIV

The Bible has a lot to say about the mind and our thoughts. Scriptures like these support counseling and helped me remain committed to the inner work I needed to do:

> Be transformed by the renewing of your mind.
>
> *Romans 12:2 NIV*

> Let this mind be in you, which was also in Christ Jesus.
>
> *Philippians 2:5 KJV*

> Casting down imaginations, and every high thing that exalteth itself against the knowledge of God, and bringing into captivity every thought to the obedience of Christ.
>
> *2 Corinthians 10:5 KJV*

To take captive every thought and imagination that sets itself up against the knowledge of God means we stop creating stories in our minds based on past experiences, especially ones that contradict who God is and that are counterproductive to who we are.

What is the knowledge of God? The knowledge is that you are chosen, royal, and holy (see 1 Peter 2:9). In others words, you matter because God sees you and has set you apart. You are special because of who you are, not because of what you do. And you are forgiven because even though you make mistakes, God offers you grace. In other words, God sees you through the lens of love and looks beyond your limitations. All of us make mistakes and have a tendency to beat ourselves up over them, but I don't believe God is as judgmental of us as we are of ourselves. You see your mistakes, but God sees you as a miracle of divine creation.

You belong to God "that you might declare the praises of Him who called you out of darkness into His wonderful light. Once you were not a people, but now you are the people of God" (1 Peter 2:9–10 NIV). This means there was a time in your life when you were trying to figure out who you are and looking for meaning without anything to guide you, other than your own thoughts and the opinions of others. You may have doubted yourself, questioned your ability, or even been uncertain about why you were born. But all of that has changed because you embraced the love of God. Now, what your Creator says about you means you no longer have to figure out life by yourself. No more loneliness, no more darkness. Praise God! Even in moments of fear, self-doubt, or anxiety, your Creator allows you to see the light of truth. The ghosts were not real and never had the power to harm you or define you. The light is truly wonderful.

Jeremiah 29:11 (NIV) says, "'I know the plans I have for you,' declares the LORD, 'plans to prosper you and not to harm you, plans to give you hope and a future.'" For much of my life I was trying to create my own plan, build my own prosperity while holding on to the fear of scarcity, failure, and an uncertain future. My hope was that success and financial wealth would soothe the pain of my childhood trauma and quiet the inner voices of doubt. It wasn't working. No matter how much I tried to create my own path, the pain of my childhood was always right there in the passenger seat and out of nowhere grabbing the steering wheel in a fit of rage, causing me to crash. The only way to end the self-sabotage was to surrender and accept the reality that I could not heal myself. I needed professional help and I needed God's guidance. I wanted to accept God's plan of purpose, prosperity, and hope for the future, but I didn't know how. No matter how much I tried to embrace God's truth, my thoughts would convince me that God has a plan for everyone, except me. Therapy helped me to heal the story I was telling myself and embrace the fact that God's word is for me, too. I learned to let go of my plan and allow myself to be vulnerable enough to trust God's plan.

Taking the opportunity to be whole—emotionally, psychologically, spiritually—can sometimes mean pushing back against church culture. My journey started shortly after my mom died of lung cancer almost ten years ago, but I was still a long way from learning how to intentionally change my behavior, when I realized the members of my church were not always helpful and could sometimes be harmful. Fortunately, I already had a relationship with God and had been involved in the church; otherwise, reactions from the church could have been a stumbling block. Testifying truthfully, from my heart about my newly overcome past, was not always met with encouragement but rather an attitude of "shame on you."

One church I attended held a Wednesday night prayer meeting and Bible study. It typically started out with a short, fifteen-minute sermon followed by testimonies—stories of what God has done in a person's life. It ended with prayer requests. Sometimes I asked for prayer, but I never had the courage to share a testimony. I didn't like speaking in public and was unsure of which parts of my story I should share. Members of the church didn't know much about my journey or the struggles of my past. It was an upper-middle-class to wealthy African American church where congregants didn't talk about growing up poor, drug abuse, and the like. A significant number of members were highly educated professionals and business owners.

One night I decided to speak up. After the sermon, the preacher asked if there were any testimonies. I let a few people go first. They shared stories of how God healed someone who was sick or in the hospital, provided employment opportunities, and blessed someone with a new car. When the preacher asked if there was anyone else who would like to share, I raised my hand. Most people there knew me, but they didn't know much about me. I told them how good God had been in my life. They smiled and nodded. I continued, revealing the challenges of my childhood: my mother's addictions, the nights I went to bed hungry because we didn't have food. I shared memories of times I panhandled to get home from school and hung out with gang members in order to protect my mom from men who were taking advantage of her. I wasn't big enough to stop them by myself, but with a crew—a gang—men who sought to use her for sex were afraid because now they'd have to deal with all of us.

As I spoke, the room was silent. I noticed some dropped their heads; others looked away. I continued, telling them I could see God's hand at work through it all, as I went on to serve in the Army and became an honor graduate in Basic Training. I gave God glory as I shared that I graduated in the top 3 percent of my military training class, went on to graduate with honors from Howard University, and landed a job as a clinical research associate while I prepared for divinity school. When I finished, I sat down. No one said a word. No clapping, as was usual for testimonies when God had blessed people with cars, homes, jobs, and good health—merely an awkward silence. The preacher thanked me for sharing and moved on.

From that day, rumors began to spread. People in church talked about my mom's addiction, how I begged people for money, grew up in the "hood," and hung out with gang members. They no longer saw who I am now, but viewed me through the lens of who I was then. People started treating me differently. Some went as far as distancing themselves and not speaking to me. Others were condescending and, for some reason, saw the need to suddenly start using slang when they spoke to me. No matter what I believed God had done to bring about change in my life, people in church viewed me based on my past, or at least felt I wasn't smart enough to hide my truth and just fit in.

Several weeks later, I told one of the church ministers about what happened and how people were making me feel because of my past. I'll never forget what he told me. "Romal, a testimony is good for the soul but bad for the reputation." I learned that the hard way. The truth is spiritually liberating, but people can use it against you. It was a painful reality.

Often in churches, a good reputation is more important than telling the truth about your journey and what you believe God is doing to change your life. That should cause you to be alert and savvy about what you share, but not deter you. Just as praise, worship, Bible study, and fellowship draw people into a deeper relationship with God, counseling should also be a key element of church life, making sure people are emotionally healthy. What's the purpose of fellowship, praising, and worshipping together if you can't even tell the person next to you the truth or be honest about who you are?

JUST DO CHURCH: "WHEN CHRISTIANS ACT LIKE CRIPS"

After the painful experience of sharing my story in church and being judged, I never told it again at that church. I did my best to fit in. I learned all the polite church sayings: "I'm blessed and highly favored"; "Too blessed to be stressed"; "God is good"; "God is good all the time, and all the time God is good." I did what everyone else did. When people asked how I was doing, I gave them the typical response that I heard others give—"I'm blessed"—and then moved on.

I was at church all the time because that was what good Christians do. I was there for Sunday service, revivals, Monday night feeding the homeless, Wednesday Bible study, Saturday Bible study, and weekday church meetings. On Sunday, when the preacher said, "God is good," I responded in unison like everyone else: "All the time." I learned "how to do church." Over time people saw that I was falling in line and learning to fit in, so they left me alone.

As time passed, I felt like a fraud. I wasn't being myself. There was more to my story. Church was a part of me, but it wasn't all of me. I knew I was hiding my truth. Where I grew up, forgetting where you come from was one of the worst things a person could do. Acting like you're better than everyone else was a good way to get your "ghetto pass revoked"—lose the respect of people in the neighborhood and forfeit the ability to return home safely. There's nothing wrong with moving out of the hood and pursuing success, but there's nothing worse than acting too good for the hood.

I discovered that the streets and church shared commonalities. Like those struggling to survive on street corners, church people engaged in unhealthy competition, dishonesty, envy, jealousy, greed, the pursuit of power, and of course, gossip. I imagined the church would be different, and when I realized it wasn't, I wondered why I should bother being in church. At least there was a code of loyalty back on the block. There seemed to be no code within church cliques. I could see the similarities between Christians and Crips (a street gang). On the street, gangs are territorial. They have their own turf or blocks they control, and they don't get along with other gangs even if those gangs carry the same name. Size is power. They love their leaders, and they only help insiders—other gang members. In order to become a member, you have to get jumped in, which is the brutal process of initiation in order to receive all rights and privileges. Churches had turf or corners they controlled. Many churches didn't get along with each other. The size of the congregation symbolized power. Members love their leaders and seem more comfortable bragging about their pastors than about God. Like gangs, some churches didn't help just anybody: You had to be a member. Getting jumped in is called baptism. Often, the church and the community are at odds; the church wants people on the streets to come inside to "save" their souls, and the community wants churches to come outside and save lives. Relationships are built on the hidden agenda of recruitment. Outsiders are not worthy of love unless they are willing to get jumped in— "saved" and baptized.

When I became a Christian at the age of twenty-four, I didn't have much experience with God or church. I relied on what I learned from others to shape my understanding of God. I didn't read the Bible very often on my own. I waited to be told what to believe when I attended Bible study or during Sunday sermons. The God I learned about operated in two extremes: punishment or blessing. If a person was disobedient, not following God's rules, they deserved to be punished. If they were good, then a blessing should be expected. The Christians I spent time around back then didn't talk much about love or grace. They wanted God to be vengeful against those who were not like them, but they also wanted God to ignore their shortcomings and bless them in spite of mistakes. The Bible was used as a weapon to work out their personal biases. It was as if they were saying, "I need God to hate you and forgive me." They beat people up with religion and reserved the benefits of faith for themselves. There wasn't much room for grace or love.

The more I sought to connect my past with the present, the more I found myself becoming distant from the church. In church, my authentic self was unwanted. The church didn't want my whole story, just the good, clean, drama-free parts. The judgmental behavior of people in the congregation felt like a tool to shame newcomers into submission.

Over time I found myself going to church less and hanging out more with friends—Christians and those who were not. I loved God, but I just didn't like church. I felt like I could finally breathe and be myself without the suffocating pretensions of church. I chose only to be around people with whom I didn't have to compartmentalize my life. People who didn't judge me for my flaws while still encouraging me to become a better person because they genuinely cared about my well-being.

FAITH AND FRIENDSHIPS

Like so many Christians, I haven't been directly connected to a worshipping congregation or a church for the last four or five years. I have spent a lot of Sundays hanging out with my friends. Some are Christian and some are not. My Christian friends are just that—we are friends, not "Christian friends." In our conversations, we sometimes talk about church, but often not. We talk about faith; we talk about religion; we talk about social justice issues. Then sometimes none of that is part of our conversation and we are just friends, supporting each other and what we're doing, concerned about how life is going and encouraging each other when life becomes hard. My Christian friends who live into a healthier authentic model of faith don't just tell me to "pray about it!" They are fully engaged in my life and they provide whatever support I need—helping me to accomplish something or recommendations or wise counsel or just making sure I am emotionally and spiritually okay.

Sometimes my Christian friends, some of whom are pastors or bishops, nudge me to reconnect with a church, but they don't judge me or force it on me. As my friends, they know my church hurt and they hold me with open hands. They anticipate I will re-engage with a congregation, that I will find a church home, and perhaps they even pray that will happen, but they are not overly critical nor are they in any passive-aggressive way trying to manipulate me back into a congregation. They are simply my friends. They've been there for me, supportive in church and out of church. That is what we do for each other…we simply care about each other.

The way we care about each other is different in some

ways because of our faith, but I engage in friendships with pastors, church leaders, or friends who just attend church in the same way I do with my friends who don't go to church. Some of them don't want anything to do with church. And for some of the same reasons I have: fear of being hurt, the negative things they hear about pastors, gossip, and people not really living their faith in a way that exemplifies love for people in spite of their flaws. They know I go to church sometimes. They know I am an ordained minister. Sometimes they joke about it. They'll tease and call me "Rev," but at the end of the day, we're just friends who support and care about each other and we're supportive.

My friends who go to church and my friends who do not go to church treat me the same. I don't have to be one part of myself with my Christian friends and another part of myself with my non-Christian friends. In all my friendships, I am my authentic self. I talk the way I talk. I am honest about my life, whether I'm angry, afraid, frustrated, or inspired and sharing my dreams. Sometimes I even cuss. (Some of my friends, who go to church and lead congregations, cuss sometimes, too!) I don't feel judged for my shortcomings by either my Christian friends or my non-church friends. We accept each other for who we are. In the words of Dr. Michael

Beckwith, "You can only be in communion with people that you're similar to."

I see my friends who don't go to church a bit differently, though. Because I am a follower of Jesus, I see them through the lens of love. I pray for them and I'll tell them I pray for them, and they welcome it. Just because they don't go to church doesn't mean they don't believe in God, embrace Jesus, or have faith. They just don't go to church. When my friends are facing challenges or pursuing their dreams, I pray for them and they will even solicit prayer, because they believe in the power of it.

Neither my faith nor anyone else's faith is defined by how many times a week or a month or a year they go inside a church building. What's important is to be a follower of Jesus. For me, that looks like living in community with people and sharing your lives with each other through the good and the bad times. This is not just a Sunday type of relationship where you would simply occupy space together, sit, clap, listen to a sermon, and go home. It's taking a real interest in each other's lives and helping each other grow into who you are truly meant to be in Christ. For me, being a follower of Jesus is about loving people without the expectation of getting anything in return. It's give of your time to help others.

Using your talents to make a difference in the world. For me, the way we live and treat others bears witness to the Gospel being alive and well. I believe that when we tell our testimonies of overcoming challenges, the stories of healing our emotional wounds become evidence that God is still in the healing business.

As a follower of Jesus, I'm more aware of the presence of God in small or simple things. I find God in a soft blowing wind. In that breeze, I feel God's presence. I find God's presence in nature or in sitting by the ocean or in hiking and getting to the top of a precipice and looking out at creation and seeing the majesty of God. I find God in conversations. Someone might say something, and in whatever they said in that moment, I could hear God speaking to me or answering a prayer or providing some type of insight and wisdom. The person doesn't even realize that what they just said resonated with me in that way. I find the presence of God in the beauty of art and life. I believe I can worship in those moments, and I can commune with God in those moments.

I spend a lot of time with my church friends and with friends who have no connection with church. Engaging in both sides of my world, of my life, I find wholeness. I feel complete. I am not throwing any part of me away. I don't need to throw away my friends who don't go to church. When I am with my Christian friends, I don't have to pretend that I don't have friends outside the faith. I don't have to hide parts of my personality or change the way I talk or the way I dress in order to maintain my friendships and be loved just for being me, unapologetically and unconditionally.

So although I haven't been in a building with a cross on it consistently, I've been very much involved in Christian life. The church is the body of believers; I've never left that. I've always been and will always be a part of that, that body of believers, engaging in relationships, being a positive part of others' lives, loving them based on who they are, encouraging them and inspiring them to grow deeper in their faith or to realize their potential. I'll always be a part of that church, and the work of that church will always be a part of me.

In order to find my faith and draw closer to God, I had to lose my religion. I realized that drawing closer to God did not mean choosing a crew—a church to attend—but living in community with people. Faith became more about relationships than religious rituals. I found myself praying more, beginning to meditate daily for twenty minutes, and reaching out to clergy mentors for advice. I've found other ways to worship God daily through gratitude and prayer. I started sharing my testimony with people in need of hope and giving regularly to religious and nonreligious organizations that address issues I had faced like child hunger, helping kids with drug-addicted parents, and young survivors of sexual abuse. I began to feel closer to God than ever before. Life became exciting again, and new opportunities came about for me to travel throughout the United States and even abroad, sharing my story of hope. The world was looking for the very thing church wanted me to hide—my honest, authentic stories of redemption.

I miss many things about church: the worship experience, music, listening to good preaching, and certain aspects of fellowship. I don't miss being treated like an outsider or being expected to act like everyone else. While I still attend church services, I only go to churches where it's clear from the way people are dressed that it's not a fashion show. People can choose dressy attire or jeans, whatever is their preference. How I am treated when I enter the building matters most, whether people who are friendly greet me and are not making a judgment about me based on my appearance, my clothes. I watch how members engage each other. Are they smiling, courteous, and conversing about life? Is everyone allowed to be himself or herself? I visit churches, regardless of denomination, where I can show up just as I am.

God wants all of us to be our authentic selves and share our stories of triumph. It's one of the ways in which people are able to see the love of God at work. My story became my message when I decided to let go of religion in order to keep my faith.

HEALTHY CHURCH

Looking back at my experiences with various churches in different cities, I realize no church is perfect; an ideal church does not exist. Yet churches can be emotionally healthy. Here is what a healthy church looks like. When I consider the pastor who sent me to anger management, I credit him for understanding the need for counseling. He was able to see issues I needed to deal with in order to become a better person. He was working to help me become healthy. A healthy church is simply one that is trying to help people become just that—healthy; it's one that is not hiding behind pretense, not pretending people are something they are not. A healthy church is aware and acknowledges that people are flawed, that we all have our imperfections, and that as a community of faith—of believers—we not only worship together but live in flawed relationship with one another. A healthy church doesn't hold people to a higher standard of living than we hold ourselves to. God so loved the world that He gave His only begotten son, so a healthy church treats people with love. A healthy church is a loving church, a community that loves without conditions, respect for pedigree or hierarchy, offering everyone grace. A healthy church doesn't label people. A healthy church acknowledges its own imperfections and meets people at their point of need in ways that empower them. A church that is emotionally healthy is one where healing takes place, where people are celebrated, respected, and honored, not for what they do but simply because of who they are. A healthy church environment doesn't have secrets. It doesn't foster or permit gossip about people. In a healthy church, people are not allowed to intentionally hurt each other with gossip or any form of mistreatment, and when it is discovered, leaders are not passive-aggressive in dealing with it but intentional and direct about letting perpetrators know that hurting people is not tolerated.

A healthy church either offers or refers congregants for counseling and speaks both from the pulpit and in private about the importance of counseling. A healthy pastor does not just preach about vulnerability, but is vulnerable.

Emotionally healthy pastors use not only the stories of others but share their own stories of their pursuit of healing and how they overcame their own life challenges. A healthy church flows from a healthy pastor. A pastor who desires emotional health leads others on a journey to be healthy and whole. Emotionally healthy pastors are trying not to be perfect, but to be their best selves.

For me, healthy churches are places that when I walk in, I don't feel I have to hide any parts of me. I don't feel I have to pretend. I don't feel I need to have my guard up, because in a healthy church, I am treated in a way that makes me feel safe. People see me, acknowledge me, and welcome me. They do not look me up and down, trying to size me up and determine if I'm worthy of respect or dignity or being treated as an equal.

A healthy church offers opportunities to engage in ministry in ways that empower people, but it doesn't "enable" them. What I mean by "enable" is they do not ignore or act like they don't see it when people are going through challenges. An empowering church creates opportunities for people to be whole emotionally, physically, financially, and socially. A healthy church honors the dignity and equality of every person. It helps them strive not to achieve perfection, but to intentionally commit to being their best selves.

A healthy church confronts its contradictions, names them, and asks for forgiveness. From pulpit to pew, it constantly recommits to the pursuit of emotional health. People genuinely try at every level. Healthy leadership flows from the top down, and people need to see their leaders modeling the pursuit of wholeness. In a healthy church, people see their leaders trying; they see their leaders being honest. Leaders of healthy churches actually share their stories rather than hide behind the cross as if they are to be symbols of perfection. Healthy church leaders are not in pursuit of perfection, but in pursuit of wholeness.

Churches that are in the pursuit of emotional health and wholeness, that are at least trying to honor and respect all people, exist all across the country in many denominations. I know a number of such churches: Trinity Church in Chicago, where Otis Moss III is the pastor; Emory Fellowship in Washington, D.C., and Pastor Joseph Daniels; St. John's in Houston, pastored by Rudy Rasmus; St. Mark Church in Taylor, South Carolina, pastored by Telley Gadson; Lilydale Church in Chicago, where Alvin Love is pastor; and Grace Church in Cape Coral, Florida, pastored Jorge Acevedo. There are many more, but these churches readily come to mind when I think about places where I walk in and am greeted by the positive energy of welcoming people. I'm sure there are other churches I don't know of that exemplify healthy nonjudgmental community. This doesn't mean these churches don't have their issues. Every church does. It means, among other things, that the topics they preach about don't just point people to heaven, but point them to wholeness. They deal with every aspect of life: Social issues of addiction, hunger, housing, and equality are addressed while also tapping into the person and helping each one deal with and confront their individual stories. In so many instances our stories are the barriers to living a life of meaning. These pastors are very transparent and honest with people, and people throughout the church are authentic. A healthy church begins with leadership that models the pursuit of wholeness and invites congregants on that journey. They remove pretenses.

I want to be a part of a church where everyone is welcomed, loved, and respected. Everyone is treated fairly and equally. Everyone is trying to make others feel safe. People encourage one another but also confront and challenge each other when they see unhealthy behavior. And they point each other toward opportunities for healing. I just want to be me in church, and I want to know that it is okay to be me, without competition or comparison traps. For me, that church is doing things differently, healthily desires to care for people, creates safe space, and holds each other with open hands, lifting one another up to become our best selves. A healthy church is willing to embrace all of me and offer grace to all of me.

That's what is important to me. I believe that is what many people are looking for in church: a place where they can stop hiding, where they can stop compartmentalizing their lives, presenting only what they think others want to see.

In a healthy church, our interactions become the evidence of what God's love looks like, what the voice of God sounds like, what the compassion of God feels like, and what God's affectionate touch feels like.

REDEEMING CHURCH IS AN INSIDE JOB

Over the course of conversations with a counselor I trusted, I concluded that my anger and my disappointment with church were because I had it wrong. I was doing the very thing that I accused the church of doing to outsiders. I was judgmental and willing to cast the church aside without any willingness to offer the church grace for its mistakes. I wanted the church to draw closer to broken people, but I was not willing to draw close to the church in its brokenness. I accused people in the church of thinking they are better than people outside, but in my own so-called enlightenment, I was acting as if I were better than traditional churchgoers. I failed to see the church the way that I wanted the church to see me. If I don't offer the church—the body of believers—the same grace that I want extended to me, I am not modeling the behavior I expect from others. I am acting like the people I condemn. How can I want the church to come outside if I am not willing to go inside? I could see my contradictions. I judged and condemned the church for its unwillingness to meet people where they are, but I was not willing to go inside and meet the people in the church where they are. Just as I thought they were hiding in the church to avoid people who are not like them, I was hiding on the streets and protecting myself from people in the church who were not like me.

People who go to church are flawed just like everyone else. Many, like me, on the outside looking in, place higher expectations on them because of their belief, but we fail to look at ourselves. Yes, their behavior sometimes contradicts their beliefs, but often so does ours. People in church are in need of grace, too. I have to view their resistance to change through the same lens that I want God to see my resistance to the hard work of changing things about myself. I've heard it said from the pulpits of numerous pastors that church is a hospital, a collection of sinners saved by grace, that God is no respecter of persons (Acts 10:34 KJV), God opposes the proud and gives grace to the humble (James 4:6 KJV), or the saying that I've heard on numerous occasions: "I may not be who I want to be but I'm glad that I'm not who I used to be." Jesus made that clear on more than one occasion and perhaps none more powerful than when He forgave a woman caught in adultery. The religious leaders wanted her to be punished. They actually believed she should be stoned, killed, and never given the chance of redemption and finding a new way forward for her life. But Jesus responded in a different way. According to the Gospel of John, "Jesus bent down and started to write on the ground with his finger. When they kept questioning him, he straightened up and said to them, 'Let any one of you who is without sin be the first to throw a stone at her'…At this those who heard began to go away one at a time, until only Jesus was left with the woman still standing there" (8:6–9 NIV). There are many lessons in the full rendering of the story as told in the Gospel according to John, but one of the lessons I think we can all quickly take away from the example set by Jesus in that situation is that you don't need a victim to validate your faith or a culprit to make you feel like a good Christian. All of us are in need of forgiveness for something, no matter how big or how small. And all of us deserve an opportunity for redemption and another chance.

Revising my church narrative was like the process of revising the narrative of my family and upbringing. Rather than seeing the church through the lens of who I was in the past, I had to re-enter the story based on who I am now. I am no longer the spiritually naive person I was when first introduced to organized religion at the age of twenty-four. I now have the wisdom of experience, the insight of lessons learned from my own mistakes, and spiritual growth that I lacked years ago.

I remember a quote from world-renowned meditation teacher Sharon Salzberg: "The healing is in the return, not in never having wandered to begin with." She was talking about meditation, but that's how I felt about going back to church. I had left the Christian congregation because I was hurt by judgmental people. I did not want to fall back into the old competition-driven performance trap where I was guided by my addiction to hearing people applaud what they deemed to be a pleasing performance. I wanted to ward off the seductive influence of becoming who other people wanted me to be in order to be accepted. I learned that the lows of church life are not times to run. I began to embrace what those experiences taught, and not devalue them or compare them to my spiritual highs or the good days.

CHURCH LANGUAGE CAN BLESS LIMITATIONS, NOT HEALING

Sometimes the language Christians—especially church leaders—use puts us at risk of enabling brokenness. What we say can be disempowering and send an underlying message that encourages others to get comfortable with their hurt, rather than trying to heal. Two of these sayings are "The church is a hospital full of sick people" and "We are all wounded healers."

These statements are only starting points. Yes, all of us come to church having, at the very least, a spiritual yearning, an illness of the soul, that can be cured only by a connection to God. And yes, many come with deep emotional wounds and need God's healing. However, if the church is indeed a hospital for sick people, then at some point, there should be healing. Without healing, the church isn't a hospital; it's more like hospice, where the best we hope to do is make people comfortable with their ailments. That limits the power of God. We do not have to go through life carrying the burden of emotional wounds. The mixture of faith, therapy, and vulnerability cure emotional wounds. God did not stop healing thousands of years ago. God is still healing today. Our testimonies are the modern-day evidence of healing, but we have to start telling our stories of emotional healing.

I embraced the concept of wounded healers many years ago when I first came into the Christian faith. I was keenly aware of my own woundedness. It comforted me to know that God could still use me in spite of my wounds to heal others. But eventually I began to question: *If I am wounded and God is healing others, shouldn't I ask God to heal me, too?* I prayed: *Give me a new testimony.* Sometimes we rely on the idea of wounded healers so much that we petition God to do things in the lives of others that we haven't even asked God to do for us. It's our badge of honor to stay broken and sacrifice our own healing for the sake of others. Or maybe we feel unworthy and believe it would be selfish to ask for our own healing. That's false piety and easily allows pride to creep in and say, "Hey, look at me, look at how much pain I'm enduring for God."

When we see ourselves as "wounded healers" rather than as "in the process of healing," we find ourselves bleeding all over each other because of unhealed wounds. People who are wounded find it very difficult, if not impossible, to offer each other healing. It's like drug addicts trying to tell each other how to stop. One person has to be healed and offer their testimony (process) of healing as a road map to the other. After the resurrection, when Jesus told Thomas to put his hand into his side, Jesus wasn't still bleeding. There was evidence of wounds in his hands as well as his side, but the bleeding and pain were gone. "Then He said to Thomas, 'Reach your finger here, and look at My hands; and reach your hand *here*, and put *it* into My side. Do not be unbelieving, but believing'" (John 20:27 NKJV).

Jesus had scars—the evidence of the resurrection and healing. Healing often leaves a scar and we have to stop hiding the evidence of our healing. We do this by sharing our stories, giving testimonies of healing, not dwelling on our brokenness. When we heal and overcome the burden of emotional wounds, our stories of redemption bear witness to the power of the resurrection. We *were* wounded and perhaps the scars are still visible, but we no longer hurt. Now we are more powerful than we were before. To paraphrase the words of the Apostle Paul, we are indeed more than conquerors through Him who loved us (see Romans 8:37 NKJV).

If the church is a hospital for the sick, we need make sure we have a big recovery unit for the people who are getting well.

THE REWARD OF REDEMPTION

Although I resist the notion that "Whatever doesn't kill you will only make you stronger," I believe those who have experienced childhood traumas and courageously dealt with them in therapy have strengths others do not have. As crazy as it may sound, doing the work of courageously dealing with my trauma has given me several gifts.

I am able to engage in conversations and hear things differently than others around me. I can anticipate what the emotional reactions of others might be in a situation, and how the words they hear might be emotional triggers. I can empathize with how a person might respond to an interaction and, in real time, right in that moment, alter the words or tone to prevent a trigger. This skill has come in handy in my role as special advisor to the president of the organization where I work. My colleague Max has said on more than one occasion that he doesn't know how I do it, but that I have a unique gift for resolving conflicts and handling tense situations with staff. It comes as a result of my own inner work.

Having to, through therapy, overcome my own emotionally challenging life experiences, learn from them, and understand their continued influence has given me sharpened skills and tools I can apply to others. The need to keep myself safe in potentially dangerous situations, growing up on the streets, gave me the ability to gauge the tone of a person's words, their posture, hand gestures, eye contact, and overall energy, and know when things were escalating. I use that information to choose my words or actions to calm things down and to determine whether I needed to leave, or prepare for a fight. These people skills and survival tools still come in handy today.

But the strength my trauma has given me most is compassion. Compassion is the superpower of successfully resolved trauma. I have done a lot of work over many years to heal the sources of my childhood trauma and there is still more work to be done, but what I have gained from my experiences of emotional pain is compassion.

The other major strength that has resulted from my trauma is control. Yes, I still carry the emotionally hurt child within me, but I no longer allow him to control my decisions, behavior, or thoughts about myself. The current me, the adult who has endured, overcome, and continually, courageously embarks on a journey of healing, is in control. It is still sometimes challenging to resist yielding to the desires produced by my wounds. I am tempted to lash out with unhealthy emotional responses to the difficulties that arise in my life. But I stay in control. I process my thoughts through the lens of who I truly desire to become. I step back and assess the outcomes of my feelings before I outwardly express them. I make better choices today than I might have if I had never started the work to confront childhood traumas and courageously deal with them in therapy.

ALTAR CALL

Many churches include a moment at the end of the sermon when people are invited to come to the altar. The essence of an altar call is the willingness of a person to come forward as a show of commitment to God and the church community. After five years away from a specific church affiliation, I sensed an altar call from God, inviting me to re-enter the life of the church. Holding on to anger and resentment because church life had disappointed me, I wanted to believe I was done with church. Church did not live up to my expectation that it would be different from the rest of society and the life I knew on the streets. But even in my anger and disappointment, I never could completely walk away from church. Although I kept a healthy distance from the inner workings of a local congregation, afraid of being hurt again, I continued to speak from pulpits across the country. I made no attempts to engage in weekly church life, because I believed people in church could not be trusted, but I attended services and felt a sense of peace when I heard congregants singing together. When the choir lifts their voices in exhortation, I can feel the presence of God and the invitation to worship. It energizes me. It gives me hope and fresh inspiration.

As I come back to church life, I do so with a new understanding. I offer the church—pastors, lay leadership, and congregants—the same grace that I have offered myself. Returning is an opportunity to have a positive influence on the lives of others because what I've learned about the love of God is not just for me. Not only does the church environment shape me, but I affect it. God's love is in me, and who I am is shaping the environment.

I'm not sure how I will make my return back into the life of a local church, but I know it's something I will do. I can't say that I will be deeply involved, like I had been in years past, but I'm open to finding a new way forward. When the time comes, I will set healthy boundaries while remaining open to the lessons I am there to learn and the gifts I am there to offer.

Jesus said He came for the sick, not the well. If we view the church as a hospital for the broken, rather than a collection of doctors and nurses, we won't have unrealistic expectations and be disappointed. We expect more of church than we do of jobs or gangs. Why? Because unlike other institution, the church calls us to love people. The Bible says "God so loved the world" (John 3:16 KJV). That's our mission statement. Other organizations and nonprofits build community, meet the needs of others, and solve global problems, but no one else does so purely because of love. That's us—the church! When we seek to be our best selves, no one can beat the church as love. The church needs to open its doors so that whoever desires to enter can do so. It gives us the opportunity to show anyone watching what love looks like.

CHAPTER 7

Vulnerable with God as Father and Honest with My Dad

I woke up to the power of therapy when for the third time in three months, my body inexplicably shut down from grief after my dad's unexpected death nearly thirty years ago. I eventually saw a therapist and the episodes stopped. To this day, I'm not afraid or ashamed to seek wise counsel whenever a significant challenge arises to threaten my well-being.

Joe Daniels, Emory Fellowship,
Washington, D.C.

My dad and I have never had a strong relationship. I didn't even meet him until I was fifteen. We first met when I spent the summer with him and his family. He has a wife and three other sons, all younger than me. That summer went fine, but a year later, I moved to live with them and it all went downhill. I grew to resent my dad. I hated him. I was angry at him for not being the father I wanted or needed. The idea of God "the Father" in Christianity and the father imagery in the church were hard for me when I first became a follower of Jesus. No one explained what viewing God as the Father means. I could not contextualize it and make it practical in my life. People talked about God as the Father, as a good father who is supportive and loving. But I also heard about God who admonishes, renders judgment, and punishes.

The language of God the Father was hard for me because my dad was not part of my life. I had expectations of my father. I dreamed of the kind of dad I wanted. Like I said, I first met my father when I was fifteen, and excluding a brief honeymoon period, our relationship wasn't great. It still isn't that great today. For years I imposed on God my own understanding of what a father is like. My view of my dad shaped who I believed God was to me. Sometimes my dad was harsh; he was also highly critical of me. At times he was just downright mean. I feel God, like my dad, would in certain situations abandon me. Or like my dad, God would not show up for me. Like my dad, God would punish me, be ashamed of me for my mistakes, or not love me because of my shortcomings. I have felt this way because of my relationship, or lack thereof, with my own father.

Early in my faith journey, I disregarded the language of God the Father. I knew I wouldn't be able to trust God in that way. Trusting God and yielding or submitting to God challenged my faith because of the experiences with my father.

Since the "God the Father" language was never explained to me and I didn't know what it meant for God to be my Father, all that imagery about fatherhood became, in my mind, either my disappointing reality with my own father or my dream of the kind of dad I wanted—neither of which is who God is.

After inner work—both in counseling and at the altar—the imagery of God the Father has meaning to me now. My view of God still comes out of my own desires for the dad I always wanted in my life, but now God not only meets those expectations, He exceeds those expectations. I see God the Father as a protector. God is a Father who never gives up on me. God the Father has unconditional love for me. God the Father sees a reflection of Himself in me; when He looks at me, He sees his own DNA, an image of Himself, and I bring God joy. My very existence brings God joy. I envision myself as a young child who sees Dad at a distance and hasn't spent time with him for a while, running up to that Father in excitement, anticipating a warm, loving embrace. God, my Father, stands there with a smile, waiting to catch me as I jump into His arms for an embrace. I feel that compassionate loving embrace from God, who adores me, loves me unconditionally. That's how I see God the Father now. God has forgiven me. God the Father is merciful. God the Father is constantly teaching me and always sees in me what I can't see in myself. God the Father is trying to guide me to avoid pain and mistakes. I'm prone to trying things my way, and when something doesn't work out, I seek God's face, coming back to ask for advice on how to get out of a situation that I put myself in and could have avoided had I just listened. At any given moment, God is ready to welcome me back home; He has been waiting for me to come back home.

Many find it hard to embrace the language of God the Father because, like me, they have some father issues. They've had father experiences that were hurtful and that need to be healed before they can accept being told: You have a new father now—your Heavenly Father.

Some do not use gender-specific language at all when referring to God; they use gender-neutral language for a variety of reasons. Some feel a male designation for God is misogynistic. The Bible says God is spirit (see John 4:24 KJV), and some interpret God's spiritual nature as both father and mother. We worship God in spirit and in truth, so I don't judge believers for their use of language and I respect anyone who takes their own journey of walking with God, abiding in God's presence, and giving language to that experience.

As I embraced my entire story and sought to heal and love myself, the imagery of God the Father imposed on me, for good or for bad, an examination of my experiences with my own dad. My typical response to questions about my dad were:

"We don't have a relationship and I don't speak to him."

"I hate him."

"I'll be glad when he dies."

Two years ago, when my friend Chan asked about my father, I was prepared to say the same things I always did. But maybe Chan knew what I was going to say, because instead of letting me answer, he told me his own story. Chan had hated his father for years. His father did not claim him as a son and was not in his life. When he heard that his dad was dying, Chan went to visit him in the hospital, hoping his father would finally say he was sorry. But he didn't. During that visit, Chan told his dad he was forgiven anyway.

Hearing him allowed me to put down my guard, own up to my feelings. I truly heard him when he told me that I needed to heal, let go of the pain and anger. When I told him about my own father, he gave me an assignment: write a letter to my dad. In that letter, he wanted me to hold nothing back—say everything I'd always wanted to say.

"Get it all out," he said. "All the anger and sadness and disappointment. Tell him about it in the letter and don't leave anything out. When you are finished, I want you to burn the letter."

* * *

My father is a Vietnam War veteran, born in the South but raised in Jersey City, New Jersey. He and my mother met in San Francisco during the time he served in the Navy. My mom was about nine years younger than my dad. My parents never married, but they lived together for a short time, and my dad left San Francisco when their relationship ended. I don't remember how old I was when they broke up. Neither he nor my mom ever told me exactly what happened. I've heard bits and pieces of the story, and from what I can gather, there was a big fight between the two of them and he left. I didn't meet him until I was in my mid-teens. He invited me to visit him, his wife, and their three sons—my younger brothers.

The day we met was uncomfortable for both of us. The drive from the airport to their home in the New Jersey suburbs was in awkward silence. When we pulled into the driveway of their comfortable middle-class home, I realized just how different their lives were from mine. Instead of the poverty and neglect I was accustomed to seeing, I saw a large yellow house on a corner lot with a manicured lawn. There was no sign of any illegal activity—no gangs or drug dealers—on their street. There was even, no kidding, a white picket fence. My father's home was, in the eyes of my fifteen-year-old self, perfect. For two weeks I played with my brothers, visited amusement parks, met other family members, and hung out with my dad. Everything seemed perfect. They were living the kind of life I had only seen on television.

When I returned to California, I didn't feel the same about home. I wanted the life my brothers had. A year later, I made the decision to move and live with my dad. I told my grandparents and they thought it was a good idea. My mom was on drugs and not around most of the time, so she wasn't very involved in my decision.

I thought life in New Jersey was going to be perfect and I would have the relationship with my dad and his family I had experienced when I visited. But living with them was different from a brief summer vacation. During the summer we were able to show each other our "representatives"—our best selves. When I moved in, the representatives quickly faded and we saw each other for who we really were. My dad saw things about me that he didn't like: I had a bad attitude, didn't follow rules, used profanity, broke curfew, and didn't like to do chores like cut the grass, take out the trash, clean my room, or do any form of work. Not to mention I enjoyed hanging out with the wrong crowd—other teens who sold drugs or skipped out on school. I saw things in him that I didn't like: He drank alcohol daily. Unlike my mom, he was functional with his drinking habit. He had a quick temper, cursed at me often, didn't spend time with my brothers or me; he was mostly a rule enforcer who came home from work, made himself a plate for dinner, and went upstairs to his room and wasn't seen much after that.

Both of us had our dreams of what life would be like together. The problem was that we weren't equipped to live up to the expectations—something neither of us knew at the time. I was a "hood" kid who took my hood behaviors to the suburbs with me. I hung out with guys who were from the streets. Guys who were hustlers, used drugs, and drank liquor. I didn't feel like I fit in where my dad lived, so I would take his car, sometimes without permission, and drive until I found the hood, where I thought I belonged, where I found people I could relate to. I would bring my newfound friends to my dad's house and leave his car smelling like marijuana. I was pretty bad. I was not the kid my dad had dreamed about. My experiences and inherited script (what I was taught and led to believe about life by my uncles) did not prepare me to be that kid.

All of us have experiential and inherited narratives, or scripts. Experiential narratives are those things that happen early in life, and because of the impact of those experiences, we carry them with us and impose them on new situations. When living in my old neighborhood, we often took advantage of other people; they were too nice—that's an experiential narrative. I imposed that belief on my interactions with people I would meet and was never too nice or overly trusting. My uncles taught me that life was about hustling, never being a follower because followers are weak, and that getting in trouble at school was cool—another inherited narrative. As a result, I didn't see anything wrong with cutting school, causing trouble in the neighborhood, or hanging out with drug dealers.

My father's childhood and even some of his adult experiences didn't prepare him to be the dad I envisioned, either. By the time he was five years old, my dad had lost both his parents within a couple of years of each other. His mom died of an asthma attack at the age of twenty-eight, and his dad died from a brain aneurysm at the age of thirty-one. His aunt in Jersey City raised him. At the age of seventeen, during the Vietnam War, he joined the Marines. Losing his parents, being raised by his aunt, and serving in Vietnam during the war did not prepare him to be the dad I imagined in my dreams. He lacked the emotional availability that would have enabled him to express love the way that I needed it. Looking back, I understand him a lot better. I understand why he was unable to give me what I needed. It was not his fault. He didn't know how. Like him, I didn't know how to be the son he wanted. I lacked the emotional and social skills to be a good kid because that's not what I was taught before I met him. Both of us made a lot of mistakes. I realize now that, as I have wanted to hear him say I'm sorry, I also need him to forgive me.

The two years I lived with him were challenging for both of us, filled with disappointments and unmet expectations. We argued often and said hurtful things. Many times, we simply didn't speak. After high school graduation, he told me he wanted me gone. He didn't care where I went, but his house was no longer my home. For years, I was angry with him for that, but I eventually understood things a bit more from his point of view. After several failed attempts to reconnect—they always ended poorly—I decided to move on with my life. I joined the Army, then went to college, and tried to live like he didn't exist. In many ways I was very much like my dad. Like him, I served in the military. Now I realize where the strict regimen and rules came from. That's what the military teaches you. I'm grateful for those rules now because the discipline I learned in the Army gave me the skills to be focused while in college. I get it now. That same discipline was what allowed my dad to build a good life for his family.

* * *

I believed my father owed me an apology. If that is the case, then I owe him one, too. I used to feel like he didn't deserve a badge of honor just because he took in a kid from the hood and put up with me. Now I see it differently. He wanted me, his son, in his life. It's something he dreamed about and longed for, but when it happened, neither of us knew how to make it work. I'm grateful for the two years I lived in his home. They may not have been great, but they were definitely better than the alternative of staying in my old neighborhood back in California. It's very likely that by allowing me to live with him, he saved my life. Knowing what happened to many of my friends while I was gone, I could have easily ended up in jail, dead, selling drugs, and never knowing what life was like outside of the neighborhood.

A story in the Gospel of Mark describes the dad I wanted and needed as a troubled teenager and reflects God the Father.

"Jesus Heals a Boy Possessed by an Impure Spirit"

Jesus replied, "how long shall I stay with you? How long shall I put up with you? Bring the boy to me." So they brought him. When the spirit saw Jesus, it immediately threw the boy into a convulsion. He fell to the ground and rolled around, foaming at the mouth. Jesus asked the boy's father, "How long has he been like this?" "From childhood," he answered. "It has often thrown him into fire or water to kill him. But if you can do anything, take pity on us and help us." "'If you can'?" said Jesus. "Everything is possible for one who believes."

Mark 9:19–23 NIV

The father in this story was determined to find help for his son. When his child had a problem, this dad did something about it. For years, his son engaged in behaviors that were harmful to his own well-being. I'm sure there were times when his dad was disappointed, angry, and maybe even thought about giving up, but he did not. The love he had for his child was unconditional, and he did everything in his power to find healing.

He took his son to the disciples; they could not heal him, but he still did not give up. The father was determined to connect with Jesus, the source of healing. When he finally has the opportunity to tell Jesus about the problem, he explains it in detail: "'Whenever it seizes him, it throws him to the ground. He foams at the mouth, gnashes his teeth and becomes rigid.'" When Jesus asked how long his son had been hurting himself, he replied, ever since his childhood. His son had been dealing with challenges and unhealthy behavior for years, but this dad was determined not to give up on his son. And even though he had hope, he still felt uncertain; even then, in the presence of Jesus, the boy's father was still uncertain. "'But if you can do anything, take pity on us and help us.'" What a deeply honest moment. To stand before Jesus admitting that he has doubts and then humbly asking for pity and help.

Jesus replied that anything is possible for the person who believes. Even then the father admits that even the act of believing is hard sometimes: "I do believe; help me overcome my unbelief!" (Mark 9:24). In other words, Jesus, I do believe, but I'm tired, and it's been so long that I just don't know anymore. I believe, I want this, but I'm not sure it can happen; help my unbelief. Right before the crowd shows up, Jesus heals the boy and helps him stand on his feet.

I was not a good kid during my teenager years when my dad took me into his home. I made a lot of mistakes. I broke promises to change my behavior. I disobeyed my father, breaking curfew, coming home late, drinking, quitting jobs, getting bad grades, and hanging out with the wrong crowd. Looking back, I can understand my father's frustration, disappointment, and even his anger. What I have had to grapple with in my inner work is understanding why he didn't believe in me. He took me into his home for two years, disrupting the life he had built with his wife and other children, but despite that sacrifice, I feel he didn't try hard enough. He didn't spend time with me. He didn't talk to me about life and what it means to be a man. He never told me that he loved me, only that I was a mistake. But then again I also get it. I remember what it was like in the military. We got yelled at and demeaned a lot. It was meant to break us down and build us back up again. The goal was to make us mentally strong. As a kid. I didn't understand that, but I can see how my dad was using the tools that were given to him. The tools that made him a hardworking, focused, and disciplined man. It would be easy to continue to focus on his flaws, but if I chose to do that, then what would it say about my own desire for people to see the good in me and not just my mistakes?

When graduation day came, I left my dad's home as he wished. I couch-surfed with friends, then enlisted in the Army, and took a Greyhound bus from Jersey City to Oakland, California. I stayed with my grandparents until it was time for Basic Training at Fort Bliss in Texas. The father I wish I had is like the father described in Mark 9: one who loved me enough to keep trying no matter how long it took for me to change.

But that Father was God. And because of God the Father's love for me, I can extend loving understanding to my father and my own children, to break the cycle of fathers who do not know how to express love.

As I continue to grow and desire to become the best version of myself possible, I realize that I can only pour out what was poured into me. My work becomes pouring into myself the values, character, emotional skills, and self-love that I missed. That's when the work of love becomes an inside job. I learn to love myself. God loves all of me and that includes my broken places. When I embrace the love of God, it gives me permission to love myself.

Learning to love myself after so many years of not even knowing what that felt or looked like has opened my eyes and my heart to see not only what I have been missing but what I was unable to offer the people I care about. I'm a dad now and I have made my share of mistakes. Like my dad, I didn't have the emotional skills and the examples to be the dad my kids needed in one way or another. I've always given voice to the love I have for my kids. The ability to say "I love you" hasn't been the issue, but the ability to express love through affection and empathy was oftentimes a challenge. Putting work and personal ambitions before spending time with my son and daughter was rooted in selfishness, not love. I lacked the skills, and I was unwilling to sacrifice as an expression of love. I cloaked my pursuit of success under the guise of being able to provide for them monetarily, and this was my justification for staying busy. Now I can see that I was driven by my ego and my desire for success and attainment. That lack of self-awareness is evident now. Like my dad, I was not there every day with my children. Over the years, I judged my dad for the fractures that created his flaws. I now find myself feeling convicted and in need of the same grace that my father deserves from me.

My children are teenagers now. My daughter, Aman, is eighteen and my son, Jordan, is seventeen. Aman is a sophomore in college and Jordan is a senior in high school. As I write about the shortcomings of my dad, I can't help but wonder what my children would write about me and how they'd reflect on the emotional needs they wanted me to fulfill. It's a humbling thought. I can't help but understand even more the need for grace and forgiveness. It's clear to me now that as much as I have wanted to hear my dad say, "I'm sorry for the emotional wounds of your past," I am not exempt from apologizing for the emotional pain I have caused others—namely, my own children. When I found the courage and humility to have hard conversations with my children about my absence and inability at times to give them the love that they needed, the beauty of redemption gave me the opportunity not only to be forgiven but to do things differently in the present.

Since my daughter has been in college, we've had the opportunity to talk more. She calls me when life is challenging, and I'm able to offer her advice or simply encourage her by reminding her how amazing, beautiful, and gifted a young woman she is. When she's sad, I'm able to listen in silent strength, show empathy, and before the call ends, do my best to make sure that it ends with a laugh or a sense that she is smiling.

I am able to tell my son, Jordan, how proud I am of who he is becoming despite my not being there for him as much as I would like. I express how much I miss him and encourage him as a young man. I have made my share of mistakes as a dad, but I keep doing the work of healing myself of my pain so I am able to break some aspects of the cycle—the generational patterns—and to show love for my children. I can't change the past, but I want to use the remainder of my life to be an example of what redemptive fatherhood looks like: the love of God, the love of self, and the love of others.

My father is still alive and at times I have tried to reconnect, but he has not answered my calls. My brother told me that on one occasion several years ago my dad wanted to stop by and see my children—his grandkids—but changed his mind because he felt that he couldn't compete with the life I have now. I was a bit hurt and disappointed, but looking back, I get it now. I don't think it had or has as much to do with competing with me as much as it has to do with perhaps some guilt or shame. The same feelings I have at times when I show up at an event where one of my kids is being celebrated for an accomplishment. There is the guilt of feeling like I did not contribute or assist them along the way—the feeling that I could have or should have been around to do more. I understand how my dad must feel now. Not to mention that I wrote him a scathing letter several years ago before I had fully embraced the process of healing through counseling. I wrote from a place of pain, not healing, compassion, grace, or love.

Chan helped me realize that whether or not my dad ever tells me he's sorry for lacking the ability to give me the love I needed, I can still be set free from my pain and anger. My actual relationship with my dad doesn't have to change in order for my inner healing around father issues to take place. I can forgive him and forgive myself for holding on to anger for so long. The beauty of forgiveness is that it frees me up to let go of the anger and resentment I have been carrying and that weighs me down emotionally. My friend Rene taught me that forgiveness allows me to choose who I want to be. It's not letting what someone did or did not do define me. If I forgive, I walk in power—the power of freedom.

Although I still don't have a relationship with my dad, I have let go of my anger toward him. I understand that my dad has been very much a part of my life. His voice was my inner critic. Since I was a "bad kid" whom my dad didn't think would amount to much, I spent a great deal of my adult life trying to prove him wrong. My desires to graduate with honors, meet career goals, and attain financial success were guided by, *I'll show him.* Funny, I never realized I couldn't show him if I wasn't even talking to him. Eventually, I had to answer an important question: What's the value of letting my inner critic stick around? Living to prove my dad wrong only kept me from living and enjoying life on my own terms. When I finally let go of my inner critic dad, a burden lifted. I felt relief.

I've learned that life isn't about proving wrong those who don't believe in us. In fact, my dad would not have allowed me to live with him if he didn't believe in me. I think he did, but he was disappointed in the person I was as a teenager. He didn't know how to help me find another way, but his work ethic and loyalty to his family set a good example. I was not paying attention nor was I wise enough to follow it when it was my turn. Life is much more fulfilling if we prove right the people who *do* believe in us. Those who believe in you will rejoice in your success and celebrate your victories. The real inner work, however, is learning to believe in ourselves, regardless of who believes or doesn't believe in us. It's an inside job. It's not a father job, although it's great to have a dad like the one in Mark 9.

Letting go of the painful memories of my father telling me that I wouldn't amount to anything and that I was an accident, when I needed him to say he loved me, was important, but so was letting go of his voice that was my inner critic and living life on my own terms. Learning to love myself helped me understand that whether he did or didn't want me does not have to dictate how I feel about myself.

I took Chan's advice and wrote the letter. When I finished writing, I printed it, got in the car, and drove to the top of Runyon Canyon Mountain in Hollywood. I had this dramatic idea in my head that I would burn the letter and release the ashes into the wind. The idea looked good in my head, but when I got to the top of the mountain, letter and lighter in hand, I realized it was a fire hazard. I drove back down the mountain, walked to a park, sat on a bench, and burned the letter. Not as dramatic as I had planned, but the same end game.

Writing the letter helped quite a bit. It was my opportunity to get it all out. I expressed my anger, my disappointment, and what I needed from him but felt I did not receive. I told him how it hurt to be told that I was a mistake. How those words made me feel like I wasn't good enough. I internalized those words, and they had a long-term impact on how I felt about myself at different times in life when I was afraid to pursue my dreams, thinking that I wasn't worthy of the life that I wanted. In that letter, I explained to him how being told that I wasn't going to amount to anything haunted me. At times when I made mistakes or failed, it was as if I could hear him saying, *I told you so, you're not good enough.* Because of his words, I judged myself; I was overly critical of myself and unable to forgive myself and try again. The fear of failure that was instilled in me because of the life-limiting belief that I wasn't good enough, or a mistake, made it hard for me to try new things. In that letter, I went on to tell my dad that I had succeeded in spite of negativity. I became an honor graduate, twice. I owned my own home, and I had a successful career. I built a life he never thought I would have or deserved.

It wasn't just what my dad had said that hurt, but it was also what he didn't say. His silence when I needed encouragement or reassurance that I was worthy of a good life and smart enough to do anything I set my mind to. It hurt to be told that I was a mistake, and it also hurt that I never heard him say he loved me. It wasn't just what he said; it was also what he did not say. His word and his silence compounded the damage that was done by my family back in California. All of which made it very difficult to love myself or anyone else.

I had a lot of feelings and thoughts bottled up inside that I finally let out through writing. Burning the letter seemed ridiculous, and although I burned the letter as I'd been instructed, I felt I deserved to have my voice heard and feelings valued. Why not mail it? I thought. My dad isn't dead. So I printed and mailed another copy to my dad. He never responded. I also called and sent him a text, but he didn't reply. When I told Chan that I did as he instructed, but I also mailed my dad a copy, he said, "The letter was not about your dad. It was about you. The writing was a purging process. The purpose was to let yourself feel and honestly share those feelings in order to release them rather than keeping them bottled up on the inside."

A few months later I was invited to speak at a church

on Father's Day. Because I had begun the process of healing the issues I had with my dad, I was able to accept the invitation. That Sunday I shared a talk I titled "Healing for Fractured Fathers." I told the audience that I did not have the relationship I wanted with my dad, that the brokenness of our relationship had been a source of pain, but I had begun healing.

I don't have to remain broken because of my parents. Even if, unlike my mom, my dad never says he is sorry, my destiny is not dependent upon someone else's apology. It's my choice to be healed and whole. I don't have to give past pain caused by others—or even myself—power in my life. My healing is my responsibility. It is not my dad's fault if I don't heal, and it is not his role to make up for what I missed in my development. Only God can be that father to me now. Writing the letter to my dad, then burning and watching the ashes blow in the wind, was the beginning of my healing. A passage in the Book of Isaiah says that God will "comfort all who mourn, and provide for those who grieve in Zion—to bestow on them a crown of beauty instead of ashes, the oil of joy instead of mourning, and the garment of praise instead of a spirit of despair" (61:3 NIV). Those are the words of a Father God.

I heard someone say that the difference between a

marathon and a sprint is how you breathe. Therapy is like stepping back, taking a deep breath, and getting some perspective. The letter I wrote my dad was filled with a lot of shaming and blaming. I wanted to get it all out, but I also wanted him to hurt, experience the sadness that I felt. Venting has its place. It allows you to get it all out. But when the intent is to harm rather than heal, it holds negative value. I vented. I let my dad have it. Yet I didn't feel better and my life didn't change. I still didn't know how to love myself or anyone else. I still lacked empathy and the courage to forgive.

If I had to write my dad a letter today, it would be totally different. I would tell him that I've learned a lot about life and love the last few years. I'd tell my dad that I'm sorry for holding on to anger and blaming him for not being the dad I wanted him to be. I would let him know that I get it now. I would let him know I understand that neither he nor I was capable of being what the other needed. I'd let him know that I am sorry I was not the son he wanted me to be. I would ask him to forgive me and say that I forgive him. If I had to write my dad a letter today, I would tell him that I now know how hard it is to be a good dad. Like him, I, too, have made my share of mistakes as a parent. Like him, I pray that my children will grow to a level of understanding and wisdom that they offer me grace and forgiveness, too. I would tell my dad that I'm a better person than I was as a teenager, that it's been a long journey, but I've finally been getting the help I need to heal the life-limiting lies I had been telling myself about who I could become in the world, that I've surrendered to and embraced the love of God, which has enabled me to love myself, love others, and love him.

I'd say, "Dad, I forgive you and I love you. I'm sorry so much time has passed since we've talked or spent time together, but I would welcome the opportunity to try again."

If I wrote my dad a letter today it would read:

Dad, I'm doing the work on myself to break a cycle for both of us and for our family. It's the cycle of emotional distance, inability to express empathy, affection, and love. The work involves being vulnerable, learning to let other people into my life by sharing my feelings and being honest about my story, all of it, not just the good, but what still hurts and haunts me. It's hard, painful work, Dad.

I'm not just doing it for myself, Dad. I'm doing it for both of us. I'm doing it for my children, your grandchildren, and for future generations so that they can be better than us, emotionally healthier than us.

Thank you for opening the doors of your home to me when I was sixteen and doing the best you could with what you had. If you had not let me live with you back then, I'm not so sure where I would be now. Your saying "yes" when I asked to come live with you was a God moment. That moment opened the door to new possibilities for me. Your "yes" led me to serve in the military and learn discipline, self-confidence, and to be told that I was smart. Dad, your "yes" to my request to live with you was the first part of the journey that led me to graduate with honors from Howard University and Duke University School of Religion. Your "yes" set me on the path to becoming the parent of two amazing children, who I thank God for daily.

Neither of us knew it then, but when you said "yes" it set me on a path to get help through therapy, learn to love myself, and write this book. Thank you for giving me a chance, for saying, "Yes, you can come live with us."

I understand vulnerability with God a little better now that I'm a dad. Vulnerability is not a sign of weakness; rather it's an expression of quiet strength. Every dad wants his children to know that they can tell him anything. As parents we desire open and honest conversations with our children. We've been through many of the things they will go through in life. We've made mistakes we want them to avoid and experienced pain we never want them to feel: the sorrow of a broken heart, the sadness of losing a friend, the disappointment of betrayal, the anxieties and fears about what the future holds. We dream and pray that our children will see themselves the way that we see them, beautiful, amazing, gifted, and special. As fathers we want to protect our children and offer guidance, but the challenge is that sometimes we don't know what's going on in their lives. We can't offer guidance if they aren't willing to share what's on their hearts.

I didn't know how to tell my dad what was on my heart. Instead I acted out, made bad associations, and expected him to do all the work in our relationship. Now I realize we fathers need our children to trust that they will not be judged when they speak, to know that they will be loved unconditionally.

And in order for this to happen, we fathers have to create safe space for our children to talk with us. We have to show them, by example, that it's okay to tell us anything. We do that by opening up our hearts to them, showing them affection, compassion, and empathy. The way we live our lives and the words we speak reveal our vulnerability to our children.

As a college student, my daughter is becoming more independent and learning to be more self-reliant. This is a time when I want to be even closer to her. I believe her journey will be amazing and full of great memories. She will also face new challenges, disappointments, feelings of uncertainty about the future, and possibly a broken heart. I want to be there for her. I want her to know that she can come to me with anything and I will love her through it.

Since she's been in college we communicate often through calls and texts. We talk about the challenges of nurturing new friendships and being misunderstood. She tells me her dreams and asks for advice. I don't just tell her that it's okay to tell me anything, but I try to model it. I tell her about the times I felt alone as a college student. I share my personal experiences of self-doubt and the moments when I felt sad or alone. I'm honest with her about the mistakes I made when I was young and even as an adult. By sharing my stories with her, she may be able to see that I understand what she may be going through. I want her to know that she's safe, not judged, when she talks with me.

On one occasion, she called me crying and angry. Her sadness led me to panic. My immediate urge was to book a flight, show up, and fix whatever was going on. She didn't need me to fix it, however, she needed me to listen. I quickly centered myself so that I could listen without trying to fix it. I helped her relax, gather her thoughts, and articulate what was going on. As she talked, I didn't listen waiting for my chance to respond; rather, I listened and prayed that God would give me the words to speak when it was time. When she finished telling me the story, I didn't provide solutions, I simply affirmed her value, I told her how proud I was of her for being herself and not compromising the person she is or her values to simply fit in. I reminded her of how gifted and special she has always been. I told her she was beautiful, amazing. "No matter what, always remember that you are beautiful and amazing," I repeated. By the time we finished the call, I could hear in her voice that she felt better. Her confidence was restored. She was focused again. I knew she would find her own way through the challenge she faced. My job was not to fix. My job was to remind her who she is and of her value, gifting, beauty, and those are constants that do not change, regardless what anyone says or does.

The more I think about what I desire from my children, the more I understand what God desires from me. I've often heard it said that since God already knows everything, what's the point in talking to God about your life? But who doesn't want to be in conversation with their child? What would any relationship look like if decisions and feelings were solely based on the idea that "He should just know already or have figured out what I need by now." Anyone who has ever dated or been married knows that way of thinking doesn't work. So why would we apply that to a relationship with our Creator? God wants to be in conversation, to know what's on our hearts, to hear us talk about our mistakes, fears, anxieties, doubts, hopes, dreams, what brings us joy, to perceive the love we have for the Almighty's presence in our lives. For us to be this open with God we must be vulnerable.

Too often we impose on God the experiences we've had with people—perhaps our fathers. When we attempted to be vulnerable, we were hurt in the process. The difference: God is love. Not sometimes, but all the time. God doesn't turn love on and off. God doesn't have issues like our parents. God isn't carrying any emotional baggage. No, that's not who God is.

God yearns to hear from each of us. God wants us to reach out without fear of being yelled at, told we made a dumb decision, scorned for a mistake, or shamed for poor choices. God wants us to be vulnerable so that we can share anything and everything without fear.

As a father, I want my children to take the risk and trust that what they share will be honored. I believe God desires the same thing. God respects who we are because God created and treasures us. Just as we must be willing to show our children what vulnerability looks like, God has given us an example of vulnerability. For me, no example is greater than the vulnerability Jesus displayed at the Cross. Trusting God the Father to the point of sacrificing His life on the cross required vulnerability. It required surrendering to the will of God. We often think of surrender as giving up or quitting. But the surrender that comes with getting vulnerable with God is letting go of our will for God's will. It's no longer resisting God's way and seeking to do things our way.

Vulnerability with God is the absence of control. Just like good fathers are not here to control our children, but to guide them, when we give up control and surrender to God, the Lord guides us. Vulnerability with God is not weakness but surrender to letting God become our strength. This is what I see in the words of Jesus in Luke 22:42–43 (NKJV): "'Father, if it is Your will, take this cup away from Me; nevertheless not My will, but Yours, be done.'" Then an angel appeared to Him from heaven, strengthening Him.

That was my role when my daughter called me, crying and sad. She needed me to be strong so she could draw from that strength to replenish her own. When we allow ourselves to be vulnerable and surrender to the will of God, we receive strength that is greater than our own. That strength allows us to live God's purpose and will.

Someone to be my strength when I am weak—that's the father I desired. It's the father I want to be for my children, despite all of my flaws. And that's the Father God is.

THE HUG THAT I'VE BEEN WAITING FOR

As I completed writing this book, I felt compelled to reach out to my dad. He and I had not talked since my mom died ten years ago. When I called the number I had for him, no one answered. I felt relieved because with every ring of the phone I could hardly breathe, anticipating what would be an awkward conversation. When I learned from a relative that my dad no longer had a home phone and was sent my dad's cell number, I panicked. I knew that if I called this time I would definitely get an answer. I was hesitant to call, and I put if off.

Days later, after lunch with a friend led to talk about our dads, I knew I needed to overcome my anxiety and make the call. My dad answered. When I said, "Hi, Dad, it's Romal!" he sounded somewhat shocked. "Romal?" "Yes, Dad, how are you?" Our call lasted about ten minutes. We talked about my kids and about my work. I was nervous the entire time.

Before the called ended, I told him I was headed to Houston for a speaking engagement the next Sunday. My dad lives about thirty minutes outside of Houston. I have been there numerous times for work the past five years, but not once did I attempt to reach out to my dad.

"You planning to come by?" he asked.

He wanted to see me. I wanted to see him too, yet I was hesitant to commit. I knew that if I said yes, I would have to keep my word. "I'll try to come by on Saturday," I said.

We continued to talk for a few more minutes and before hanging up, he said, "I hope to see you on Saturday."

During the car ride there, I experienced all kinds of emotions. I gazed out the window at the highway. My memories were of the first time I went to New Jersey to see my dad when I was fifteen. I felt like a kid again, nervous and uncertain what to expect. I started feeling angry as I remembered challenges in our relationship during the two years I lived with him. I thought, *He's old now; I can take him in a fight.* I wanted to be angry when I saw him but I knew that was not right, that that's not who I am now. I had to focus my thoughts on everything I learned in therapy, the person I desire to be in the world, who loves others, showing grace and compassion. I vacillated from sadness to anger to the kind of man I aspire to be. My mind was so unsettled that I fell asleep.

About five minutes from my dad's house, I woke up, called, and told him that I'd be out front. He greeted me at the door. We hugged briefly and went upstairs to the sitting room where he had been lying on the couch watching television. I sat as far away from him as I could. We kept the conversation light.

Eventually, the anxiety I experienced in the car was gone. I was not sad, angry, or anxious. I was fully present. I felt good. At one point when he sat back down on the couch, I sat with him. I looked across at him and I felt different. I no longer saw him as the intimidating angry person I remembered. I just saw my seventy-two-year-old dad. I felt compassion and love for him. I interacted with him, not as a child, but as the man of faith I am now, a man on a journey of healing who is able to offer others grace. I no longer felt the need to bring up painful old memories. The past was resolved by living as the man

I am now, letting go of the thoughts and feelings of the wounded child I once was. The way my dad talked to me and treated me, I felt respected and valued. We didn't settle the past, but we enjoyed the present.

When the car service arrived, my dad walked me to the door and we stepped outside. "Dad, it's cold out here, you should go inside," I said, feeling genuine concern for him.

"I'm okay," he said.

Not saying another word, we turned to each other and hugged. He kissed me on the cheek and said, "I love you."

"I love you, too," I replied, "and I'm sorry it took so long."

Our hug was brief. My dad is worse than me with hugs. If I have a three-second rule, then he has a two-second rule! Funny thing is, I wanted to hug him longer. I wanted to over-hug my dad. I wasn't uncomfortable and I didn't count the seconds.

I could see him smile slightly as he turned and walked away. He was happy, and so was I.

After I got in the car I felt energized, with a new sense of peace. An emotional weight had been lifted. I felt proud that I was able to do something I wasn't sure I could do. I had proven to myself that I am not trying to become a better man, I *am* a better man.

During the ride back to Houston I reflected on our hug. *I actually wanted to hug my dad!* It didn't freak me out. I thought my discomfort with hugs was because of the incidents growing up. I'd healed from that childhood trauma enough for three-second hugs. My father held the key to another level of healing for me. He held the key to my ability to appreciate the emotional connection of a loving embrace. That's the hug I had been waiting for!

God is a Father we can be vulnerable with and surrender to, so that the Almighty can be our strength.

CHAPTER 8

Men Friends—
The Three-Second Rule

Discovering who we are, what passions and fears drive us, and how we interact with this uneven world may be the most important journey any of us will take. The irony is that this journey toward our authentic self cannot be taken alone. Looking for help along the way reveals strength.

Brian Miller, pastor, Aldersgate Church,
Montgomery, Alabama

Until recently, hugging men made me uncomfortable. I felt like my space was being violated. I still don't like the pat-on-the-back hugs, because they make me feel like someone is trying to burp me like a baby. I have categories of hugs. First there is what I call the athletic hug, which involves shaking hands while at the same time offering a quick embrace and then you release.

Then there is the church hug. Most people are familiar with the church hug. It's a polite side hug where both people intentionally avoid allowing any "private parts" to come in contact with the other person. The key is to approach the other person sideways to signify that you're coming in for a church hug and it's safe. There are also the over-huggers. These are the people who don't know when to let go. They like the affection of a hug. Last but not least is the almost never necessary hug that I like to refer to as the "stranger danger." This is the full-body, chest-to-chest embrace; completely unnecessary under most circumstances unless you have just been rescued from a natural disaster or a burning building, then it becomes the oh-my-God-I-made-it-and-I'm-glad-to-be-alive hug or, the survivor hug. Other than that, for me a full body hug is stranger danger.

I never know how long a hug should last. To establish boundaries for hugging, I used to have a three-second rule. When a man would hug me, I would count to three and then let go. It made hugging a little easier because I could set the terms for how long the awkward moment would last, and three seconds were plenty.

I have consistently had challenges building healthy long-term friendships with men. Reflecting on issues I have as an adult, I understand my childhood and my current behaviors, thought patterns, and feelings are connected. My upbringing and situations in my youth had a lasting impact on my adult life. Early in counseling—soon after the Mr. Breakfast incident and my therapy session with my mother where she apologized—I learned to acknowledge my pain, to change how I understand what happened. I knew I couldn't change what happened, but I could change the way I *chose* to remember it. I had to change what I kept telling myself *today* about what happened *yesterday*. But some things I would not even let myself remember. I pretended they never happened.

Journaling helped those pushed-down memories emerge. One night while writing, I realized that part of the reason I had trouble with men friendships wasn't due to my relationship with my dad. It was due to a couple of traumatic childhood experiences where I was almost sexually abused as a boy—on two different situations. First by an older man; I got lucky and got out of that situation. The second time, by a young adult; I am guessing he was somewhere close to twenty years old and I was maybe twelve years old. I had completely forgotten about those experiences. I had repressed them; they didn't exist to me.

Then one evening while writing, I asked myself why

I have such a problem with building healthy long-term friendships with men, why it makes me uncomfortable when male friends say "I love you" or something like that. I have two adult mentors who love to hug. They are extroverted, compassionate, affectionate, and give uncomfortably long hugs. When each one hugs, he will say, "I love you." Every time it would freak me out. The hugs were just too long. I call people like this "over-huggers."

As I said, I used to have a three-second rule on hugs. Get in there and count one thousand one, one thousand two, one thousand three, release. Up to three seconds, I was not very uncomfortable, but after three seconds I was.

I was so uncomfortable that I did some research on hugs. One article pointed out that in order to receive the full emotional impact and power of a hug, it should last twenty seconds. Now that is a long time! Twenty seconds of someone hugging you. I considered that cuddling, not hugging. It is supposed to make you feel a sense of connection and affection.

I wrestled with hugging and questioned why I was so uncomfortable being hugged by men who had mentored me, and hearing affectionate language from them. I had long disagreed with and shed the cultural dynamics—

expectations of black males and what affection should and should not look like if you are a strong black male. I knew it was foolishness, but I still wrestled with my discomfort until I traced back my challenges to those two childhood experiences. Almost being molested is the root of my distrust of other men. The past attempts of those men to take advantage of me lay buried, hidden even from my own memory.

Later, when I asked my therapist why I forgot about these experiences for so long, until writing triggered them, he explained that certain traumas are so difficult that in order to protect itself or to protect you, the ego will repress them. To remember them could lead to devastating results in your life. He used a lot of therapy language that I understood simply as my memory was protecting me. My brain had sealed off those memories in order for me to be okay. The problem was those memories were still in my adult subconsciousness, and I still lived them out, unbeknownst to me.

DON'T TOUCH ME THERE AND DON'T TOUCH ME LIKE THAT

Shortly after that conversation with my therapist, my girlfriend Marchet and I were sitting next to each other and she put her hand on my leg and squeezed my inner thigh near my knee. She had been doing this since we started dating and I had never had a problem with it, but out of nowhere this simple gesture of her touching my leg when we were sitting together and squeezing my thigh toward the knee area made me really uncomfortable. I had a knee-jerk response (no pun intended), got angry, grabbed her hand, and said, "Stop doing that. Don't touch me there."

"What's wrong?"

"I don't like it when you touch my thigh that way."

"What is the problem? I'm just being affectionate. I'm just touching you. What is the big deal?"

I couldn't respond. I didn't know what was going on at first. I just knew I didn't like it.

She was upset, too. My lack of explanation, which she saw as withholding information, probably added to her distress. This was new behavior. Marchet reminded me that she'd always been affectionate toward me and touching my thigh was not new, but my response was. It made her uncomfortable. For her, it felt like rejection. We were out of the country when it happened. She had joined me on a delegation to Havana, Cuba, for work. Standing on a corner waiting for a streetlight to change, after the incident, she was visibly angry. When the light changed, she started walking away from me.

"What's the problem?" I asked. "Why does it anger you so much that I'm telling you something I don't like? I'm trying to communicate."

She turned around with a stern look on her face and in a firm voice said, "Because it's new and I don't like it."

In that moment I learned a very important lesson. In a relationship, new behavior is not cool. Whatever you start doing at the beginning of a relationship, you're going to have to ride out, keep doing that behavior. After two marriages, I should have learned that, but it became extremely evident that day on a street corner in Havana.

Marchet is an amazing woman. She is an introvert with extrovert tendencies. Like me, she prefers time alone, but when around other people, she's affectionate, empathetic, and loving. One of her love languages is compassionate touch. Squeezing my thigh, just above the knee, was not sexual; it was one of the tasteful, non-verbal ways she let me know we are connected, that she is there and fully present with me at a given moment—at a dinner or an event. I had always appreciated her compassionate touch. Prior to these new feelings of discomfort, her touch made me feel valued. Her touch was something that let me know she was there for me, that

I wasn't alone. In the past, when she touched me, I felt a sense of connection that wasn't just physical but emotional. It made me feel proud, secure, and even confident. I used to find myself instinctively reciprocating her behaviors by touching her hand or shoulder. I'd never been that expressively touching kind of guy before Marchet. Other than a genuine response to her leading, I can only attribute it to the healing process that came with therapy. I was intentionally trying to do relationships differently. I now adopted behaviors that aligned with the caring and affectionate relationship I previously longed for but hadn't had because I never committed to changing how I related.

After these memories of my childhood were triggered—by the writing process and talking with my therapist—my interaction with Marchet changed.

I didn't yet fully understand my reaction and couldn't give her any explanation. She found it hard to break the habit of doing something that used to be fine and now was not. We were getting into arguments about it, although when we argued, we would resolve it rather quickly. Sometimes we wouldn't even talk about it, but we both felt that brief silent treatment. It just didn't make sense to her, and I couldn't make sense of it myself. I just knew I no longer liked that touch. It became such a disruption in our relationship that I spent some time thinking deeply about it. She was right. Ever since we had been together, she was always affectionate in this way. She always touched me that way. *Why am I so conscious of it now?* I asked myself. *Why is this disturbing me so much?*

Then I asked myself one of the questions I learned in counseling: *When was the first time I felt this way about someone touching my thigh?*

My memory flashed back to a childhood experience. One night my mom had gotten home late from a night out drinking. She was drunk and called me at my uncle's house at two o'clock in the morning. "Come home!" I had to travel across town to our apartment. I had to take three buses to get home. One stopped directly in my uncle's neighborhood, near his apartment. I would take that bus through his neighborhood, down the hill to the next bus stop, hop on another bus, take that bus for about fifteen to twenty minutes, get off that bus, and then finally get on a third bus. This third bus stop was in a warehouse area. At this time, way past midnight and well before even a glint of morning light, I was standing there by myself at the bus stop. I was in the sixth or seventh grade; I know this because we were living in the Mission District and I was in junior high school, probably my first year. Standing there, waiting on the bus, I was scared. It was pitch-black and so quiet, an eerie quietness. I could hear rumblings in the factory areas and around the warehouses. I was on the alert in case someone came around the corner and tried to harm me. I was there, a kid, by myself in the middle of the night.

A car pulled up. It was a burgundy marque with a white top. The guy stopped the car. He had a curly Afro, dark skin, glasses, a goatee, and a mustache, neatly trimmed. I was looking and wondering, *Why is this guy stopping?* He rolled down the window and asked, "Do you want a ride?"

Of course I said no. "I'm waiting on the bus."

He said, "Well, are you sure? It is going to be a long time before that bus comes."

I remember thinking, *He is right. It is late and I don't know when this bus is going to come.* It already felt like forever. I just wanted to get away from those warehouses.

He said, "Come on. I'll give you a ride; I'll take you home."

So I got in the car with him. I gave him turn-by-turn directions to get to my house. This is pre cell-phones, pre-GPS, pre–Map Quest; none of that existed. As he followed the route that I had told him to take, I began to feel a little more comfortable. *This is going to be okay,*

I thought. About ten minutes into the ride, he asked my name and where I went to school. I told him. Then the energy shifted, and out of nowhere he started rubbing my inner thigh. I got nervous. I didn't know what to make of it. I didn't know why he was doing it. I just knew it made me uncomfortable. I no longer felt safe and began to think fast, *What can I do?* Typically when in danger, I would call my uncles, so I said their names: "Do you know big Moe and little Moe?" I asked the man.

He immediately removed his hand from my thigh and put his hand back on the steering wheel. "Yes, I know big Moe and little Moe," he said. "Why?"

"They are my uncles," I said.

"Oh, those are your uncles?"

"Yeah, their sister is my mom."

He didn't touch me anymore and he continued to follow my directions. We got to an area near my apartment where there was a bread factory. I knew how to get home from there. I knew all of the ins and outs of the neighborhood. I thought, *If he lets me out of this car, he will never catch me.* I didn't want him to know where we lived because, by then, I was afraid of this man. As we approached the bread factory, I said, "You can let me out here."

No apartments were right there so he asked, "Are you sure?"

"This is good. I'm fine. Let me out." I jumped out of the car when he pulled over, wondering if he could tell I was afraid when he let me out. I raced through an alley before getting to our street, to make sure he didn't know where I was going and wasn't following me. I waited until there were no cars and then I ran up our street and into our apartment building. When I got upstairs, of course, my mom was passed-out drunk. I went to my room and never brought it up except to my uncles later on. I told them what had happened. They asked me to describe the man and the car. But they never mentioned it again, and neither did I.

The experience of that man, that night, grabbing my inner thigh, I now revisited when my girlfriend, who wants nothing but the best for me, touched me. One of the first times I felt unsafe with an adult male came back, evoking that very same unsafe feeling, such a threat that I grabbed her hand and told her not to touch me there.

As the memory came into focus and I let myself look back on it, I began to understand my reactions. I sat down with her one day and said: "I think I know why I am uncomfortable with you touching me on my thigh like that." I told her what happened.

"Oh my God. I'm so sorry. I didn't know. Thank you for telling me and I won't do that anymore," was her response.

It felt good to have that conversation with her, to be courageous enough to tell her. I wanted to tell her because I care about her. I wanted her to understand me, and to know where my behavior is coming from, so that we can strengthen our relationship. I invited her into my story, even the parts of it that aren't pretty. She has at times invited me into her story and things that have not always been the best experiences. In sharing that time together and that honesty, I felt safer and more connected to her. She understands a part of me that she didn't know before, and now she is able to respond in a way that affirms me and affirms her love for me. Because she is affectionate, every now and then she will still squeeze my thigh above the knee and she will catch herself and stop. But rather than lashing out, I will just hold and rub her hand; she'll know what that means. Or she'll say, "I'm so sorry I did it again." And I'll smile and look at her and say, "It's okay." I am becoming able to dissociate her current actions from what happened to me years ago and receive her touch as affectionate and caring—as she always has been. I know I am worthy of that and I value that from her.

Sometimes I attach behaviors, feelings, and emotions to ways people treat or interact with me now that are not based on the current moment. I associate those interactions with a past, unhealed story. I am now able to revisit those stories and disconnect the present moment from that past history. I can re-engage in ways that are healthy, that build connections.

Today, I'm a better hugger. It took some work to find the cause of why I have been so uncomfortable with male affection. I am able to receive the hugs from my male adult mentors and hear their words "I love you" and receive them. Now I am even able to say "I love you," too. Oddly enough, I actually feel more like a mature grown man when I do express words of love for my friends. I get it now. There's nothing mature, grown, or healthy about being afraid to say "I love you" to a brother you care about. It is not weak, feminine, or sexual; it is a verbal expression of the bond of brotherhood, loyalty, and a friendship that is not just based on hanging out from time to time watching sports, drinking a beer, or cracking jokes. My friends I have who are mature enough to express love for me are men with deep family values, character, and loyalty. Our friendships are solid. We are there for each other during the good times and the bad. We are vested in each other's lives. Men like Paul Hosch, Robert Lee, Joe Daniels, Vance Ross, Rudy Rasmus, Marc James, and Michael-Ray Mathews. These are my friends—I love them, I would go to battle for them, and I know they would do the same for me.

Still, letting male friends get close to me emotionally was a major challenge. I have kept up an emotional wall to prevent men from getting close enough that they could hurt me. As a result, it has been very easy for me to sever ties with men friends. When I sought to find the source of my inability to build emotional connections with friends who genuinely cared about me, it triggered other traumatic memories that I had pushed deep down inside. I started examining experiences that had shaped me, to learn from them, and if necessary, seek to heal them so that they no longer would have a negative influence on my life.

I was probably in the sixth or seventh grade when it happened. I wasn't yet living with my grandparents, but I visited them almost every weekend. Normally, when I arrived at my grandparents' house, I'd find my neighborhood friends playing outside, but that day no one was there. I went to a few friends' homes where people would typically hang out, but no one came to the door. I decided to try Brian's house, a kid my friends and I used to play football with, but we rarely if ever were invited to come to his house.

When I knocked on the door, his older brother, who was around eighteen years old, answered. He told me everyone was out shopping but would be home soon and that I could come in and wait. When I sat on the couch, he offered me something to drink and returned from the kitchen with two glasses of juice. While I drank my juice, he sat close enough to make me uncomfortable. I told him that I would come back later. When I stood up, he grabbed me and wrestled me to the ground, attempting to unbuckle my belt. I grabbed the buckle and would not let go. We tussled for a few minutes, but I didn't give in. Finally, he shoved me in the back and yelled at me to get up and get out. As I was walking out of the house, he said, "You better not tell anybody." Afraid and confused, I walked back to my grandmother's house in silence.

NOT MY FAULT

These experiences were pivotal memories influencing my ability to trust male friends. I lived much of my life unable to build strong connections out of fear that someone might be trying to take advantage of me. I questioned if any male figure could be trusted and always kept up a solid emotional wall.

When I shared the trauma of almost being molested twice with my friend Juanita Rasmus, she reminded me that when I was a child, I was not in charge, I had no control over the situations, and they were not my fault. But as an adult, I now have agency and wisdom, and I choose the people I let into my life.

The most important thing I had to remind myself of with each experience of sexual trauma is that they were not my fault. Redeeming the self-worth, confidence, and courage those moments sought to steal—so that I can be a man who trusts other men enough to be friends—I have to know it wasn't my fault. I repressed the memory, silenced my inner voice out of fear that I must have done something wrong, and as a result, blamed myself for what happened. I've listened to people share similar and even more difficult experiences of sexual abuse, who either blamed themselves or made excuses for their abusers. None of us is to blame for the behavior of those who inflict physical and emotional harm and who rob us of our innocence. We are not responsible for their actions, neither were we collaborators. We were not in control. We were children or adolescents. If it happened to you, it wasn't your fault.

As a child or youth, what happened was not my fault. As an adult, however, redemption is my responsibility. That experience does not have the power to hurt me now. Rather than live in denial and act as if it had never happened, I must choose to be aware of how the experience could influence my behavior and treatment of others. I have to make a conscious effort to control my thoughts and manage my emotions so that I do not hold others responsible for what someone else did. I have to do the work so that I do not allow my wounded places to keep me from knowing what genuine affection and love feel like.

COURAGEOUSLY VULNERABLE

Vulnerability terrified me for much of my life. It opened the door to be hurt. But it also opens the door for so much more. It offers the opportunity to love and be loved. Vulnerability is the freedom to feel deeply and have empathy. It allows us to receive the comfort and security that come with knowing you are deeply loved and cared for without an agenda.

Vulnerability draws us closer to God. It requires that we lay down our armor and surrender to the yearning of the soul to be free from the weight of pretending that we are in control. Vulnerability requires that we are honest about our feelings. Whenever we are unapologetically honest about our feelings and the internal desire to be cared for, we draw closer to God, the source of all truth.

Today I am learning to be courageously vulnerable, and that means opening myself to deeper friendships with men. Courageously vulnerable may sound like a contradiction, but it's not. Because I was afraid of vulnerability, it required courage to give it a try. As I revisit past pain, I am redeeming the power that it took from me. Childhood traumas attempted to steal my ability to give and receive healthy displays of male affection, take away my ability to trust men, and rob me of the opportunity to give and receive love from them. Each of us deserves to know what it feels like to give and receive true agape love and the comfort of affection without an agenda. We deserve it and we must be courageous enough to seek it. To be courageously vulnerable requires owning the power and agency that we have as adults. We must be mindful of the past but never let it dictate the present. We choose not to be held hostage by past pain. Instead, we can redeem the past by exercising the courage to be vulnerable with people who have earned our trust. By doing so, we are able to experience the healing power of genuine love and affection.

To be courageously vulnerable means we let go of the thoughts, judgments, fears, and emotions that want to impose themselves on us. As Richard Rohr once told me, "We become the courageous watcher, where we step back and observe our inner selves without judgment. Our feelings are not us because we are not forever living our past."

Over the last year of working on this book, two of my uncles died: Roy, the youngest of my mother's four siblings, and Glenn, the oldest of them all. I also lost a very close family friend, Willie C. All three died of cancer in the last twelve months. Of the people who were a part of my upbringing, I have only two left, an aunt and uncle. I've never experienced so much loss in one year. The most recent loss was my uncle Glenn. I found out on Facebook. It was 5:30 a.m. and I was preparing to head to the airport on my way to a speaking engagement when I checked social media and saw the post by one of my younger cousins. It was too early to call. I was on my way to speak, so I suppressed my feelings of sadness to get through the day and the talk I had to deliver.

I am very much an introvert and have a pattern of keeping to myself, especially when I'm sad. Normally I would just stay alone with my thoughts. Rather, I sent my "uncle by choice" Rudy Rasmus a text that my uncle had died. Rudy called me and in the course of our conversation said, "Romal, allow yourself to have a friend. Call Mark Lomax; he's a good brother." I broke from my normal isolation and took Rudy's advice. I sent Mark a text and asked if he was available for lunch. I told him what was going on. We talked about life, how I was feeling, and we even laughed. It was therapeutic to let someone in, to be willing to share. I felt better, and most important, I wasn't alone. I allowed myself to be vulnerable without feeling the need to just carry it all by myself. Rudy was right—sometimes you just need to give yourself permission to have a friend, let someone in, and talk about how you're feeling.

FRIENDSHIP IS ESSENTIAL TO THE SOUL— FRIENDS AND FRENEMIES

"Hey, Romal, I know a lot has happened over the last year, but I really miss our friendship. Maybe all of us can get together sometime."—Lance

Lance and I became friends just a couple of years into me becoming a Christian. We hit it off quickly. He had also served in the military. Both of us felt a little out of place in church. We still had a little street edge about us and church was different. We talked and hung out often. We understood each other and would share the challenges we faced in church and life. At times we referred to each other as brothers.

When I was going through my first divorce, I pushed most of my friends away. I assumed they would be judgmental and gossip behind my back. Some did. I chose not to risk being vulnerable, which didn't allow them to be a source of strength during a time of great emotional pain. I was conflicted about friendship. By definition, I believe friendship to be a person's ability to develop a close bond built on mutual respect, encouragement, trust, honesty, and emotional support. It requires being you, emotionally vulnerable without fear of judgment or being seen as weak. Friendship requires courage and risking hurt. I did not want to take that risk. As a result, I pushed Lance away the same way I had pushed everyone else away.

We are created with the innate desire for connection or relationship with others. Knowing that we are cared for and matter to the people around us is what makes us feel alive. Without the deep sense of connection, of friendship, life can feel empty. Nurturing authentic friendships feeds the yearning of our souls not to be alone. I definitely felt a sense of loss when Lance and

I were not as close as we once were. Looking back at my friendship with Lance, I feel that it would have been worth it to take the risk to allow him and others to be there for me when I needed them most. Unfortunately, I'll never know.

To my own detriment, I have held friends to a street code—similar to the way I once viewed the church. Growing up, my uncles taught me that the first rule of the streets was never trust anybody. Everyone has an agenda, and being too trusting was a sign of weakness. The weak were easily exploited for money, drugs, or power. Information was power that would likely be used against me. I learned to approach everyone with suspicion and always assumed there was an ulterior motive to kindness. I told people only what I wanted them to know. I shared the parts of my life that I was willing to let people into, but I always kept the most vulnerable aspects to myself.

I used the same street code with Lance. An old narrative was guiding my life, and I convinced myself that he could not be trusted. I told myself that if I let him get too close, he would take advantage of me. As a result, I was alone and in a twisted way resentful that my friend did not try harder to be there for me when I needed him.

I treated friends like Lance as potential enemies or what some call "frenemies." The walls I put up to keep people out left me isolated and alone. They became my personal prison. No one knew "the real me." I was hiding the parts of me that I sought to protect—my fears, doubts, and insecurities.

I've learned that I can't ever know if a friend is willing to be supportive and accept me as I am unless I am willing to tell them my truth. Trust cannot occur until I am willing to open up to others and create opportunities to build trust. Only then do I see what people are made of and who they truly are in my life. Fear of betrayal and manipulation results in friendships that are less than authentic. My belief that men friends could not be trusted had nothing to do with others but everything to do with me. I couldn't be trusted to be honest and authentic and therefore I was suspicious that others were faking it, too. Even if someone, like Lance, was genuinely trying to be a good friend, I found it difficult to trust because deep down I knew I was not being a truly genuine friend to him. I was hiding the parts of me I didn't want him or anyone to know.

FROM VICTIM TO VICTIMIZER

When you don't confront the pain of your past, you run the risk of becoming the very thing that you've been running from. The narrative I inherited from my family members—people cannot be trusted—made it difficult for me to build deep connections because I chose to accept those narratives as true. My experiences of abuse by men reinforced what I was told by family. Until I questioned my memory and became courageously vulnerable, I was an adult who lived in the past and in pain, in a life filled with contradictions.

When I was a child, people always left when I needed them the most. As an adult, I was the one leaving. I found myself still yearning for community but unable to connect. The reality is that I would never be able to find what I wanted until I was willing to create it within myself. Feeling like I belonged and believing that I mattered to those around me had nothing to do with the actions of brothers like Lance and everything to do with what was going on within me. Finding what I was looking for was an inside job. I had to do some work on myself and redeem what past pain and trauma took from me. Connecting the past with the present has allowed me to see which beliefs and experiences have guided my behavior, then find a new way forward. I had to heal what was going on within me before I embraced the people and relationships around me.

The way I interact with men in work or casual interactions has evolved over time. I think some things come with time and maturity while others are certainly due to the benefits of therapy and doing the inner work of emotional healing. In my twenties, relationships with male friends were deeply superficial. Everything was about partying, drinking, hanging out, and sports. Neither I nor my friends at that age took much of an interest in what was going on in each other's lives beyond fun. I had older friends who saw our friendship as more than just entertaining and genuinely cared about me as a person. In my thirties, my friendships were still superficial. Most of my friends at that point in my life wanted something. Life was about business and making money.

I had a number of friends who exploited my friendship for connections, ideas, or access to opportunities. I was aware of those relationships and I tolerated them. Sometimes it was mutually exploitative; the friendships were for power and information to climb the ladder of success. Character and integrity were negotiable. "Friendship" was a term people used loosely. It didn't mean any deep connection or loyalty to a person, just that you knew the person. You could name-drop that you were friends, but relationships were shallow and lacked meaning. I felt the same way about male friendships in church. Beyond three or four guys that I hung out with often, friendships with men at church felt superficial, rooted in class stratifications based on where they lived, who they knew, where they worked. Church friendships with men were probably the most gossipy I've ever experienced in my life. I wasn't used to that from men, and it made me very uncomfortable. Where I came from, gossip was dangerous. If word got back to the person you were talking about, that person was likely coming to see you so that you could say it to his face, and it was probably going to get physical.

Often friendships were competitive. I compared my life to theirs. Comparing and competing between friends made it hard to celebrate each other. When I got my first book deal, I told someone I considered one of my closest friends. We would talk several times a week and had known each other for at least ten years. When I said, "A publisher accepted my book!" he didn't say congratulations or that's great news; his response was, "I didn't even know you were writing a book." That was all he said. When I purchased my first home, another friend came over to see it and, instead of congratulating me, proceeded to point out all of its flaws. When my book was published, still another friend made this passive-aggressive compliment-noncompliment, "I see your little book is doing well." These were the kinds of men I chose as friends and who chose me.

It would be easy for me to say that my male friends were not caring and supportive, but the hard truth is that neither was I. I attract who I am, not who I think I am or pretend to be. If you want to know who you are, look at your five closest friends. That will show you who you are. I attracted the kind of person I was.

Following male leadership has always been a problem for me. The person who cared about me most and I loved more than anyone in the world was my grandmother. My grandmother always believed in me. She encouraged me to move in with my dad because she knew nothing positive would come of staying in the neighborhood. I didn't have many consistently positive examples in my life, men to help me make good decisions. So as a young adult, when men tried to provide leadership, I would reject it. I didn't trust that they had my best interest at heart. I believed they were only trying to tell me what to do or use me.

My views about life, friendship, and male leadership have changed with maturity and therapy. In a sense, going to therapy is a sign of maturity. My values have changed. Life is now about meaning and doing what will add value to the lives of others who will outlive me. My friendships are a reflection of my values and the kind of person I desire to be. I choose my friends based on what they care about, how they treat people, and their willingness to be authentic and honest. Today my friendships are not competitive but connections around shared values and holding each other accountable to being our best selves. Friendships mean loyalty, trust, and being supportive through good and bad times, not just when the friendship is convenient.

LEADERSHIP REQUIRES VULNERABILITY

Therapy and vulnerability with God have helped me redeem the self-worth, confidence, and emotional security that I lost and have made me receptive to male leadership. I no longer assume male authority figures are exploitive and dictatorial, but rather may offer guidance and want to teach me something. Letting go of the beliefs about myself and about men that shaped me, I've learned to trust and respect good male leaders. The more I learn the power of vulnerability, the more I find it safer to respect and trust authority. Being vulnerable enough to follow and respect authority does not mean that I am giving up my power; it means that I am strong enough let someone else operate in power without feeling like doing so takes away mine. Submitting to authority and allowing my older male friends to offer guidance, hold me accountable, and check on me to make sure I'm doing okay have given me something that I've always wanted—to not feel alone in the world. Friendship is indeed essential to the soul.

TIME WAITS FOR NO MAN

Lance died several years ago in a motorcycle accident, and we never had the chance to rekindle our friendship, although we tried. It was mostly my fault. If I had to choose one friendship that I wish turned out differently, it would be my friendship with him. I would tell him that I'm sorry for neglecting our friendship, for not trusting him, and not admitting that I was afraid of being judged. If I had the chance to do it all over again, I would tell Lance that I needed his friendship because I was sad, alone, and could use a friend who was loyal and trustworthy.

The missed opportunity to be friends with Lance again challenges me to be courageously vulnerable with the people in my life now.

CHAPTER 9
Broken Men

My therapist says that she is my compassionate witness. She sees my life from the inside out—as very few people do. She offers grace when I judge myself harshly; she offers concrete lifelines when I am sinking. The stress of responsibility can easily wear me down. My therapist helps ground me in my true self.

Monica A. Coleman, author of Bipolar Faith,
Los Angeles, California

One day while scrolling through social media posts, I came across a video from a series JAY-Z did on men and love. As I listened to the stories of men—celebrities as well as guys who were not household names—I connected to the theme: Regardless of their backgrounds, success, or socioeconomic status, none had been taught how to love. As men, we are taught all kinds of things about work, responsibility, success, and sex. But we're not taught how to love and not given many examples of what love looks like. Many of us grow up confusing love with sex. Love requires vulnerability and empathy. Those character traits are not typically taught. We see few examples of these qualities in men. They are often seen as female characteristics. As I listened to these stories, I thought: *Wow! So many broken men!* Our emotional being, ability to love, capacity to accept love are all broken. How can we be whole if we were never shown the way, or given the chance to learn? For me, wholeness as it relates to being a man and a friend is about the ability to live a non-compartmentalized life. Wholeness is about allowing yourself to feel—to be sad, angry, afraid, or happy—and not have to hide those emotions out of fear they make you appear weak. Wholeness is about being a man who's comfortable in his own skin and strong enough to embrace every aspect of who you are as an emotional being. As a man, you don't just show your friends your representative—the person you want them to think you are—but you're able to show them all the aspects of what makes you, you. To be a man who's whole means you don't pretend to be strong when you are weak and allow your friends to be your strength. It means that when you're afraid or uncertain, you allow your friends to be courageous for you.

If I wanted to have friendships that withstood the test of time, I had to become a person who didn't quit on people. If I wanted friends who would be there for me (even if I made mistakes), I had to be willing to forgive others when they made their mistakes. I was pretending to be emotionally healthy, but I was still broken, and broken people attract broken people, or in my case with Lance, broken people can't even recognize wholeness, can't give good relationships a chance. I had to examine and confront the experiences that shaped the kind of friend I had become and undo the impact they were having.

In my own upbringing, childhood and adolescence, I cannot recall a time when I felt whole, when there wasn't some form of chaos or disturbance or disruption. I was born into a single-parent household, so from the day of my birth, out of the gate, wholeness was not offered to me. The only time I was probably whole was when I was in the womb, when my mom was pregnant. But given that she was seventeen, my dad was in the military, and they were not married, she was probably experiencing some stress even during the pregnancy.

Perhaps the only wholeness available to me, or to anyone, is the journey to wholeness. Once we're here—the day we are born—a sense of wholeness comes from a relationship with God. The deeper and deeper that relationship with God grows—the more we submit, are vulnerable, open, and surrendered to God—the more we draw close to God and the more we experience what it feels like to be whole.

Perhaps I was not broken. None of us are actually broken, because to be broken requires starting out whole in the first place. How can something that was never whole in the first place be broken? I started out as pieces of my broken parents and added more pieces throughout my upbringing—childhood, adolescence, and adulthood. Rather than regretting that I am broken, I can pick up those pieces and begin the process of creating something whole.

BROKEN PEOPLE BREAK THINGS

The more work I do to heal from the pain and trauma of my past experiences, the more I become aware of people I've hurt. Due to my own pain, my own issues, I have caused others pain and sadness. Broken people break things…friendships, relationships. As much as it has been important for me to heal, I have been a part of other people's lives and part of their pain. They have bad memories of having dated me or been in a friendship with me. I was broken and didn't know it. They weren't even aware of my brokenness and let me enter their lives, assuming I would do no harm. Even I had no idea that my trauma would show up in those situations.

I can't simply heal without acknowledging that I have been the source of someone else's pain. When I identify my pain, hurting others is part of that pain. That is a humbling feeling. The humility that it brings, the empathy I desire from others, reminds me that I have to be a person who is able to empathize with the feelings of others. For some people in my life, empathizing with their pain means dealing with the reality that I caused it. I can't heal, recover from my trauma, and look at my bad experiences without coming to this realization: I also hurt someone. That causes me to embrace the love of God even more. It draws me closer to the heart of God. As much as I need to forgive the people who hurt me, I need to forgive myself, and I also need forgiveness from the people I've hurt. Knowing how much it meant to me when someone like my mother, who was the source of my pain and trauma, acknowledged it through an apology, I realize that the same is required of me, too. Telling the people I've hurt due to my own pain, "Oh, I was living in trauma or I didn't realize how much my past was influencing my present," doesn't go far enough. My desire to be healthy and to be a whole man requires that I say, "I am sorry." I acknowledge that in this book. Maybe some of the people I've hurt will read it, and if they do, this is my moment to say:

"I'm sorry. I apologize for the pain that I've caused. There is no excuse for it. I wish I had known then what I know now. But knowing what I know now, you deserve an apology, and I deeply regret that I caused you pain. I'm sorry for the mistakes that I've made that hurt you. I feel remorse for my bad choices and my bad behavior, and I am seeking to be forgiven, not just by you, but by God. God, forgive me for the mistakes I have made. I am conscious of them now. I wasn't aware then and I now see the impact they had on You, and I honestly feel sorry. For those who look back on their time with me, and the memories are not good, you deserve an apology. What better way to do it than to acknowledge it in this book, which will outlive me."

Healing is not one-sided, not just about me. It is about others who I am a part of; I have been a part of their lives.

At times, I have been man enough to engage those I've hurt and apologize to them. I've even sought out people I felt I owed an apology and, many years later, apologized. It had been years since some of the experiences that caused my pain happened, as in the case of my mother, but the latter-day apologies I've received were still worth it. Acknowledging my wrong and connecting with people I've hurt were not necessarily to re-establish a relationship, but to simply say, "I'm sorry and I hope you will forgive me." It matters to their healing just as much as it matters to mine. Engaging in the healing of those I've hurt builds some integrity into our relationships, even if just for the moments of the apology. I can be my authentic self, the person I am today, if I apologize in genuine honesty.

Broken people certainly break things. People like me who have lived for years with brokenness, and been the source of pain for others, engage this journey of healing confronting what has harmed us *and* acknowledging the harm we have caused. We do not use the fact that we were broken or hurting as a cop-out for our bad behavior, but we own our bad behavior and admit those we hurt deserve an apology. We are courageous enough to go back and revisit the pain we caused and offer them what they need for healing, whether they forgive us or not.

Many men like me were not taught how to love, be vulnerable, or express their feelings. I saw evidence of this in the JAY-Z video where men were talking about the challenges they have with women and relationships. In order to become the kind of man you desire to be, a man who is whole, a man who is tired of breaking things, we have to do work inside ourselves. It's an inside job.

To become whole means when we don't know how to love or express our feelings, we find courage to learn, to be vulnerable enough to admit that we lack the emotional tools we need and get help to develop those tools. That means going to therapy, and absolutely nothing is wrong with or unmanly about going to therapy. It's the smart thing to do. It's what a "real man" is willing to do. As mentioned in chapter 2, in "Why Men Don't Go to Therapy," a man who desires to be whole is not concerned with what other people will think, but with what he will think of himself.

I admit—and have shared my story—that going to therapy is hard. God and therapy go together. God makes it possible to take that first giant step to therapy. God is the essence of love. Renew or begin a relationship with God through prayer.

Prayer is simply a conversation with God, an honest conversation, no pretense or fancy language required, and hood-speech tendencies, including poor enunciation, are what God prefers, if that's you. Talk about your hurts, emotional bruises, wounds, failures, anger, and uncertainties with God. Present them to God. Even though God already knows them, you need to be honest about your inability to fix yourself and admit that you need God. Ask God to give you the strength to do your inner work, to be your strength and guide, and to send the right people into your life.

While you're talking with God, request power from the Almighty to take steps to let the wrong people go. Becoming whole requires an honest look at the people in your life. Look at your five closest friends and be honest with yourself and with God about what those relationships reveal about you. Seek out men who are the kind of man you want to be. Be honest about the emotional walls that you have put up in order to avoid being hurt. Sometimes the walls we build to avoid being hurt also keep us from being healed.

Just as I've shared my story with you, revisit the stories

that have made you the person you are today. Honor those parts of you—good and not-so-good—by forgiving yourself and forgiving others so that you move forward without the weight of blame, guilt, or shame.

Learn how to love by letting God love you first. From God's love, you'll learn how to love yourself and then love others.

CHAPTER 10

Badges and Burdens

On more than one occasion Pastor Dennis Black-well strongly encouraged me to see a therapist after my divorce. I finally stopped resisting and I am so glad that I did. The process of healing through therapy gave me new life.

Vance P. Ross, director of Annual Conference Relations, Discipleship Ministries, Atlanta, Georgia

My first sexual encounter had already occurred several years before either of the incidents of attempted sexual abuse I shared in chapter 8. My first sexual experience was when I was ten years old. My family was out shopping and I was left with the babysitter, who was eighteen. That day she asked me to come into the bedroom and lie down. She climbed on top of me and we had sex. I didn't really understand what was happening, but

I knew it was sex. Afterward she laughed as if it was fun and told me not to tell.

My family returned and everything else about the day was normal, as if nothing had happened. Later while my babysitter was still at our home, I went to use the bathroom. She was in there combing her hair. When I walked into the room, she was shocked: "What are you doing!" she cried. "Get out of here before someone sees you." I was confused, given what we had done earlier. It was in that moment that I began to think that it was probably bad.

A few years ago, I told a female friend about what happened with my babysitter. I was bragging about my experience; I thought I was a sexual prodigy. She sat silently for a second and her facial expression appeared sad. "Romal, that was rape. When a girl does it to a boy, nobody seems to care; it's as if the boy is just becoming a man. That's the problem. I'm sorry that happened to you."

I had never thought about it that way, but she was right. It was rape.

I grew up in an environment where male identity and machismo were defined by two dominant characteristics. The first was the ability to fight. The second was sexual prowess. Sleeping with different women was something to be proud of, a rite of passage into adult life. It was as if sex made you a man.

My uncles were very sexually promiscuous and dated a lot of women. They set the example I sought to live up to. When I was in the eighth grade, I invited my girlfriend over to watch music videos. My plan was that we would have sex. Nothing actually happened, but while we were lying on the floor in front of the television kissing, one of my uncles came in and saw us. The next day he made up a story that he caught us having sex. I was embarrassed, but my uncles joked about it and seemed proud of me. Their behavior reaffirmed that sexual promiscuity was condoned and celebrated as what makes a boy a man. Since being sexually promiscuous was permissible behavior, I was not taught self-discipline, abstinence, and knowing when to refrain.

What was a badge of honor during my adolescence became a burden, symptomatic of another broken place within me: I was unable to communicate affection without sexual intimacy.

YOUR MATE IS NOT SUPPOSED TO BE YOUR MOM

From the day I received my mom's letter telling me she was off drugs and in church, our relationship was completely different from my experience growing up. Our conversations were pleasant. She was sober, her mind was clear, and she was concerned about what was going on in my life. My mom prayed for me daily. Mom sent toys for her grandkids, called me regularly, and visited one Christmas. Things were different in this new chapter of our relationship. I finally had the mom I always wanted.

A few years into our newfound relationship as mother and son, my mom called one day, and from the sound of her voice, I could sense that something was wrong. She told me that she had cancer and the doctor gave her a year to live. I was shocked. I told her that I wanted her to come live with me and she agreed. It took several months to make the arrangements, and I then flew home to California to meet with my mom and her doctor to discuss treatment and the process of relocating her to Maryland. I arrived on Tuesday, she died on Wednesday, I buried her on Saturday, and I went back to work on Monday.

My mother's death forced me to think about my life. I remember sitting in the middle of the kitchen floor one night at about two in the morning, crying. I remembered my mom, her addiction, and the challenges we had during my childhood. My life had become so different as an adult. I had served in the military, received degrees from two universities, owned a home, and had a good job. My life appeared to be different, but I had to admit it wasn't. My family didn't have the skills to love me the way I needed it as a child, and all these years later I still didn't know how to love myself. I definitely didn't know how to love my wife or how to let her love me. On the outside everything looked good. I went through the motions of love, but on the inside the places of my emotional pain were still unhealed and the yearning of my soul for love was unfulfilled.

As I sat on the kitchen floor of my first home—proudly purchased only a year before my mom died—I reflected on the community I'd come from, the nights I went hungry, and the days I had to panhandle to get home from school. All the memories of living with drug-addicted family members—the verbal abuse, the rejection, and loneliness—flooded my thoughts. "Who am I?" I asked myself. I'd buried so much of my past in order to succeed, be respected, and treated as an equal among my peers that I didn't even recognize myself anymore. I felt my life was a lie because no one knew the real me, or the stories that shaped who I had become. I had presented myself in relationships, including with my wife, as who I wanted to be and not who I was. She

knew some of my stories, but neither I, she, nor anyone else knew that I still didn't love myself. I treated my
wife, the person who was supposed to be closest to me,
like she was no different from anyone else. I was distant,
not affectionate, very narcissistic. I lived my life trying to
fix myself with public perception and money. I believed
that what the world thought of me could fix me. *If people
like me, I will like myself*, was my thinking.

I didn't let people know that my drive and my pursuit
of success were rooted in the fear of poverty and never
having enough when I was a child. I didn't admit that
constantly looking for the next achievement was motivated by trying to prove to myself that I'm good enough
and I matter. I didn't let the people around me, including my wife, know that my inability to nurture and
maintain closeness actually stemmed from my fear of being rejected. I was terrified of being thrown away in my
relationships with women because I grew up feeling like
I never came first to those who were supposed to love
me—my family.

Sitting on that floor, crying, I could no longer ignore
the internal struggles that I was hiding. Suppressing the
memories was no longer good enough. In the pain of my
loss after my mother's death, I finally got honest with
myself about what I wanted most. More than anything

else, I wanted to put an end to the internal struggles that haunted me. I wanted to stop pretending to be happy and actually be happy. I wanted peace of mind, and that was going to require dealing with what was going on within me and no longer being distracted by the pursuit of things around me. The happiness I longed for was an inside job.

From that day forward, expensive clothes, shoes, cars, and other symbols of success—which are often the badges a man presents to women—took on less meaning to me. What I wanted most was to learn how to love myself. I decided to stop hurting and find healing. I was tired of harming others and myself in relationships. But in order to do so, I needed to do more inner healing. The life-limiting stories that I accepted as true had shaped my relationships with women so much that I was self-sabotaging the family life that I wanted, by holding on to old beliefs that were no longer good for me. I realized that the only thing keeping me from having the relationship I desired was me. I knew I needed a way to reconcile my past and my present.

As I continued in counseling, I learned that the solution to that challenge of unifying my past and my present could be found not by hiding my story but by looking at how it was still impacting the person I had become. My past mattered, all of it—the good, the shameful, and the awful. It doesn't define me, but it is part of me. And so I started at the beginning, looking at my past again—all of it—to see what it could teach me about relationships, finding what I needed to keep and what I needed to heal and leave behind.

One key area I had to examine was how I viewed and related to women. By the time my mother died, I was on my way to a divorce from the mother of my two beloved children. And despite years of counseling, I married and divorced a second time. But I kept trying to get it right. I am now in a healthy relationship with my girlfriend, Marchet—who blesses me, even when I rebuff her for touching my knee, right above the thigh.

Every aspect of my life, including marriage, was guided by trying to prove that I was worthy of respect and love. Focusing on achievement was to prove that I matter and get women to affirm my value. After my mom died, I was depressed. At the time, I thought the source of my depression was my mom's passing. But I was also wrestling with my own identity in relationships with women. I wasn't sure who I was anymore. The depression and anger were part of the revolt led by the aspects of me I chose not to love. I had been hiding part of me, and a part of my soul was dying. I wanted that part to be known and set free.

Losing my mother ignited a conflict within me and forced me to realize I was not relating in ways that honored my truth. I had suppressed the experiences of my childhood. I hid those things from myself and any women who came into my life. I thought suppressing bad memories was required of me as a man, especially a man accepted by society and church. I felt women would not want me if they knew the real me—the parts of me I thought were shameful, awful, and ugly.

Every relationship I had with a woman ended in a breakup. It had nothing to do with them and everything to do with what was wrong with me. As yet another relationship was ending, I reached out to a friend. I was sad and needed someone to talk to. I was frustrated, tired of dealing with heartache, over and over again. I needed help figuring out what was at the root of my relationship issues. I called my friend Tashion. She knew my personal story and my relationship history. During our conversation, she said, "Romal, you keep looking for your mom in your mate. But your mom was not meant to be your mate and your mate is not meant to be your mom."

In my search for a loving relationship, I was trying

to find someone to give me the love I wanted from my mother. I went from one dating relationship to another, hoping to find something I myself did not have the ability to offer—love. I developed a pattern of falling in love quickly and over time distancing myself, out of a fear of abandonment. When one relationship ended, it wasn't long before I dated someone new. I didn't like being alone. Being alone forced me to live with my internal emptiness and seemed to prove I was not good enough. I needed a relationship in order to feel like I mattered.

From Tashion's words, I learned that no relationship could give me what I was not willing to offer myself first. I was no longer a child. What my mom did not give me during my childhood, I had to learn to give myself now. Past pain did not have to define my current reality. If I wanted to be loved and offer love in return, I had to learn how to love myself. I had to believe that I was worthy of love simply because of who I am and not for anything that I have or do. I only came to believe that I was worthy of love when I got vulnerable with God and accepted God's love for me. I had to surrender, let go of my constant striving to earn love, and simply accept that I am loved. When I began to experience my Creator's love for me—based on nothing but my existence as God's creation—I started to have glimmers that

I might feel worthy of a woman's love because I loved myself first.

AM I WORTHY OF LOVE?

"Romal, you don't have any roots. I always did my best to love you, give you a sense of home and family, but it did not seem like that was what you wanted," were words a former girlfriend shared with me on more than one occasion, and for the last time, when we broke up.

She was right. I don't have any roots. I've never experienced a sense of place or felt as though I belonged. Much of my adult life has been spent searching for something, but I never knew exactly what that "something" was. I thought love was something I could go out and find, something that could be measured and obtained. Love was about actions and what a person did for me. Love was not about mutual feelings or my own deep connection with another person. What I felt was love was actually more superficial, self-serving. Authentic love is neither. Adrianne was trying to show me that love is about a deep sense of connection. The connection precedes any action. True love sees you for who you are, not what you have or who you might become.

I recognize now that I have been looking for proof

that I was wanted, that I mattered. That proof would give me peace of mind, a feeling of security, and assure me I was going to be okay. That I was worthy of love meant I could actually receive the love I longed for: love I could trust, love that would not betray or harm me, love that would not end in disappointment.

"Until death do us part" is how I felt—*not* about my marriages or relationships with women—but about my inner pain! My pain and I were married, together forever. That vow needed to be broken if I ever wanted to truly live and love. If I did not stop my past from controlling my emotions and thus guiding my behavior, I would die without the love that brings purpose, meaning, and knowledge of who I am truly meant to be. The emotional wounds of my past were a barrier to healing and the reason for my loneliness.

EMOTIONALLY UNAVAILABLE

Like I witnessed in my two years with my father, I spent most of my time focused on work. Achieving goals and pursuing success were my ways to feel worthy of love. I kept myself busy to avoid dealing with what was going on inside me. Glorifying the idea of being busy with work was, in hindsight, my way to avoid dealing with being emotionally present in a relationship. I projected my insecurities onto relationships by pushing women away to pursue goals and accomplish more. What I wanted to have in life, which I felt attracted women—things I wanted to buy—took precedence over the kind of person I wanted to be. I was emotionally unavailable, distant, and distracted.

To understand emotions is the most difficult challenge of doing this inner work—this inside job—of getting vulnerable with God. For me, it's like talking about astrophysics. They both sound extremely complicated, and because they sound complicated, I've ignored my emotions for much of my life. I know feelings exist and I'm aware that I have them, but I'm just now beginning to figure them out. Apparently emotions are pretty significant in a relationship. They're the air that breathes life into it. I guess I've been holding my breath for years.

Several years ago, at the end of another failed relationship, I was reminded of my uncanny ability to suffocate a relationship by holding back my feelings. When this relationship was ending, my girlfriend's words were, "You're a good person, Romal, you just aren't emotionally available." I typically blew such statements off as what I tagged as "syndicated conversation" lines I'd heard on more than one occasion, which were by now

like an old television show that I had seen before—
syndicated. I typically chalked them up as the woman's
problem, believing it was her, not me. But this woman's
parting words stuck with me.

Most of my relationships started out fine. I was excited about each woman I dated. At the beginning, I
always felt emotionally safe. But eventually, in each relationship, I found it difficult to share how I felt...even
after years of counseling and relating to God taught me
how to identify my feelings. I was unwilling to be vulnerable to a woman. I always had my reasons for being
distant, and I shared them with no one.

Sometimes the distance was the result of thoughts I
conjured up in my head: *This relationship will be ending
and I'll end up being alone again, so I will not express my
feelings or let her know that I'm hurt. I don't want her to
know she has that much power in my life. I'm strong and
I'll be fine. No woman is going to treat me any better than
my mom, and she abandoned me.*

Other times my insecurities produced the distance: *I
am not good enough for her. When I was a boy, no one ever
put me first, so no woman, especially a good woman, is going to put me first now that I'm a man. I'm just not good
enough for her, like I wasn't good enough for my mom.* I
never told any of the women I dated about the thoughts

that controlled my emotional distance. I didn't tell any woman how she might help me feel safe. I didn't even know what I needed. I just knew I was afraid to get too close emotionally.

It was a rare occasion in the course of all my relationships when I said "I love you" or offered words of affirmation like:

> "Girl, I'm down with you like four flat tires."
>
> "I'm glad you're in my life."
>
> "I feel so grateful that you're with me, that you chose me and I'm good enough for you. I never thought a woman like you would choose me, but I'm glad that you did. I feel special that you're with me."
>
> "You're an amazing woman and I'm blessed to have you."
>
> "I'm willing to open up my heart and my life to you."
>
> "I want to do whatever it takes to make you feel safe, secure, beautiful, wanted, and loved."

To be honest, I didn't even know what "emotional availability" meant until I Googled it. After wading through articles and websites, I discovered that emotionally available people find strength in giving and receiving words of affirmation, comfort in sharing themselves, and compassion for others. I, on the other hand, conformed nicely to the descriptions of the stereotypical person struggling with emotional unavailability: critical, self-involved, emotionally guarded, uncomfortable expressing feelings and being intimate.

Broken relationships with women and the inability to experience the love I longed for created a cycle I kept repeating and I didn't know why. For a long time, I didn't want to know why. I just chalked it up to being "damaged goods from the hood."

As I got closer to God and began to love myself— even the parts of me that emerged from my ugly, painful, shameful stories—I was forced to deal with the source of the problem. To give up on the idea of ever knowing what love is also meant giving up on fully loving myself. I learned that I have to know that God loves me before I can love myself, and the evidence that I love myself is being able to accept love from someone else. I had always been looking for proof that I was wanted, that I mattered, but that proof didn't come from receiving the love I longed for. It comes first from giving the love I risk receiving.

Learning to love yourself gives you the ability to recognize love from another person.

Perhaps one of the biggest signs to me that I am becoming a more emotionally available person is my willingness to cry. I learned as a boy that men don't cry. In the past, I would never cry in front of a woman. I thought it made me appear weak. I no longer feel that way. Tears are powerful; they open the door to release pain and let peace come in. Tears can be the baptismal waters of deliverance. Tears wash away the scabs of an old wound so that it becomes a healed scar and no longer hurts.

Recently I was sitting up late one night talking to my girlfriend, Marchet. We were talking about her parents, and she asked me to tell her about what happened when I lost my mom to cancer. It's a story that I rarely tell. As we lay there on the couch holding each other affectionately in the darkness, I began to tell her the story of what happened in those final hours with my mom.

I arrived Tuesday morning. My mom was in the hospital and I went to see her. The plan was that we were going to meet with her doctor, discuss her treatment, and then on Saturday, I would take her back to Maryland with me. We met with the doctor and he told me she had about a year to live. We discussed if she wanted a DNR (do not resuscitate) order. She said yes, that if she were to go on life support, it could only be long enough for her brothers and sister to come and see her, but then I had to let her go. We agreed and I told her there was no need to worry about it because we had a year. The doctor left the room. My mom and I continued to talk. She was in a lot of pain. Her chest was hurting as she breathed. She prayed and told God that she wasn't afraid to die, but she just wanted the pain to stop. I sat there feeling powerless and wishing God would stop the pain. Mom was tired and wanted to rest. I told her that I was going to head back to her apartment and get some sleep. The five-hour flight from D.C. had worn me out. I told my mom I'd be back in a few hours. That was a Tuesday evening.

At this point while I was telling Marchet the story, tears slowly began to roll down my cheeks. I was getting to the part of the story that required real vulnerability and courage. She sat quietly and listened.

I told Marchet that when I got back to Mom's apartment, I took a nap. But instead of sleeping a couple of hours, out of nowhere I was jolted out of my sleep, deep into the night. I looked at the clock and it was 2:00 a.m. I was terrified that I had left my mom alone all that time when she probably needed me.

I picked up my phone and I had several messages. She had been calling me. When I listened to the messages, she was clearly in pain. It sounded like she was struggling to breathe. I'll never forget listening and hearing her say, "Romal, please come. Hurry up. I'm so scared. Please come."

I rushed to the hospital. When I arrived, she was on life support. I was devastated. I felt I had let her down, left her all alone. I stood at the side of her bed and said, "I'm sorry, Momma. I'm here now. It's okay. I know what you want me to do." Mom was beyond consciousness. Our conversation from earlier the day before about the DNR felt surreal. I didn't think we would face it for at least a year, but it was here now. At this point I was sobbing as I told Marchet the story and so was she.

I told Marchet that when I left my mom's room, I went outside to the hospital parking lot. I felt alone with no one to help me. I called a few preachers who were friends and told them what was happening. They encouraged me to be strong and told me that I was not alone. After that I called my uncles, my aunt, and my cousins. I told them to come; my mom was dying and they needed to come to the hospital to say their good-byes.

As the sun began to rise, family started showing up. They waited outside my mom's room, waiting for me to instruct them. I said, "You can go in and see her, and after that, I am going to have the doctor take her off of life support, because that is what she told me she wanted."

We gathered in my mom's room and prayed. After everyone left, I stood by my mom's side holding her hand. A friend was on the phone with me saying, "Keep talking to her, she can hear you. Tell her how you feel, say what you need to say, let her know she is loved." I did as my friend said and we got off the phone so that I could have some final moments with my mom. I leaned over to whisper in her ear. I told her that it was okay to go. I told her that I loved her, then kissed her on the cheek and forehead.

The medical team removed the life support as I stood there holding my mom's hand. The doctor was across the room completing paperwork and asked me to come sign something. The moment I let go of my mom's hand, the heart monitor went flat with a loud and long tone. Mom held on until I let go of her hand, then she was gone.

I lay across Marchet's chest crying. She continued to listen and I said, "I still miss my mom so much," and cried aloud while she continued to hold me.

That's what receiving love, what vulnerability, looks like for me now. In my past relationships, before I did the inner work of connecting with God and confronting my past, I was unwilling to share, feel, cry, and admit how I feel. Rather than owning my truth and trusting a woman to hold me with open hands, I feared judgment or being perceived as weak and could not see the value in being open and free to be the real me.

After telling Marchet that experience, she said, "Thank you for letting me in." We cried ourselves to sleep. Good tears. Loving tears. The tears and vulnerability made us even closer than we were before. The next day, she told me she felt our bond was strengthened because of that conversation. I felt the same. Something felt different. She knew a part of me, a part of my story, that I hadn't liked talking about because it revealed my fears, sadness, and guilt.

ABANDONED PEOPLE ABANDON PEOPLE

There is a saying that "hurt people hurt people." I believe abandoned people abandon people. When I was a kid, the people who were supposed to care for me typically walked away. As an adult, I did everything I could to avoid the pain of someone leaving me. Because of my unresolved abandonment issues, my marriages didn't have a chance. From the moment I said "I do," an hourglass was turned and it was only a matter of time before I walked away. For me, the vow "to love and to cherish, to have and to hold, until death do us part" were words

that meant "good enough for now." I sabotaged relationships with emotional distance and infidelity. Admitting
it is hard but it's true. I was not good to myself and unable to be good for anyone else.

The only way to stop the cycle was to understand the
impact on my life of my mother's burdens as well as the
badges of sexual prowess I learned from my uncles. My
mother consistently chose her addiction over me. Those
choices instilled in me the belief that I don't come first.
When she would not come home after work and I had
to fend for myself to find food, it was ingrained in my
psyche that I had to rely solely on myself. When she
would go missing for days without even a call, while I
stayed with my grandparents, the belief formed in me
that she was not concerned about me. From these
experiences, I held the belief that my life and well-being
were no one else's responsibility but my own, and I held
this frame of reference as truth with every woman who
entered my life. Love, I believed, was, at best, temporary
and often conditional, for just like my mother, any
woman who cared for me would eventually leave me.
Experience with my mother had convinced me that
eventually any woman with me would decide I wasn't
good enough and move on to someone better.

I was trapped in a cycle of beliefs that made it feel

natural to sabotage relationships. I was distant so if a woman left me, I wouldn't be too attached—like I was to my mom—and it wouldn't hurt too much, like those times Mom left me. I took care of myself first—before taking care of anyone else—because from my childhood, I didn't believe anyone else was concerned with my well-being. I viewed every woman in some way like my mom, putting herself first, and my needs were, at best, a distant second. That's what I chose to believe. I acted on those unexamined beliefs and never fully committed to any woman because of fear and distrust. When I felt I was becoming emotionally connected to a woman, I built walls to keep my feelings inside, to keep myself safe from the hurt that so deeply wounded me as a child.

The emotional walls I constructed to keep from being hurt prevented me from experiencing a deep connection to the women in my life, and hence, healthy relationships. It was as if when the pain of my past spoke to me, it said, *What I, your pain, have taught you is all you need to survive. Remember your pain and how I have motivated you to succeed. Love? You don't need the love these women are trying to offer. It's not real and will only end in pain like it always has. The problem is not you, it's them.* The voice of past pain that dictated my life was often subtle in its deception and persuasive with its logic.

But when I listened to it, the brokenness that guided my choices always left me stranded on an island, alone, blaming everyone else for my isolation.

The walls I constructed to protect myself from pain, which kept me emotionally distant from women, also lured me away from God, Who is the very essence of love. Opening myself to God's love and doing the hard inner work of therapy revealed to me that the wounds of my past were manipulating my subconsciousness into a false sense of self. I had to either do something or attain something to be worthy of love. I'd spent so much of my life as an overachiever, thinking that once I have enough, I'll be enough. Then I'll get the love I want from a woman. Yet nothing filled the void. I always ended up alone. I had made my marriage vows with the brokenness, low self-worth, and belief that love relationships are rooted in doing, rather than being. I had engaged in every relationship with a false sense of self.

The emotional wounds of my past were a barrier to healing and the reason for my loneliness.

GETTING LOVE RIGHT

Every aspect of my life was based on my need for control. Even as I started the work of healing, I was still trying to control the outcome. My assumption was that if I did the inner work, then I would eventually feel loved. Inner work was to achieve a result. Healing from my life-limiting childhood beliefs was another goal. I had to learn that although doing inner work is good and needs to be done, it is not a means to an end. During one session with my therapist, he said, "You don't do the work to receive love; you do the work as a result of knowing that you are already loved by the divine—God."

Although I was letting down the walls I'd built as a result of emotional insecurity, I replaced them with another wall, a form of control: the belief that my inner work would result in being loved.

Understanding the beliefs that created the cycle of broken relationships was only the first step in finding a new way forward. Making up my mind to do better because I knew better was only the beginning. I tried forcing myself to trust, feel, and let a woman in, but eventually the unresolved trauma of the past would creep back into my behavior. My behavior remained a by-product of my life-limiting beliefs about myself that I projected onto women. I did a lot of reading and talking to people who use meditation practices to find balance, and I learned that old beliefs and patterns could be resolved only if the stories were examined—as I had done—*and* replaced with *new* beliefs and patterns. Changing beliefs takes time, discipline, patience, and a willingness to offer myself a lot of grace along the way. But even self-examination and forming new beliefs and patterns still wasn't going to be enough to let love in. I also had to be courageous enough to be vulnerable.

Although I longed for connection and love, my walls would not let it in. Walls don't just keep pain out; they keep love from getting in. My walls never kept me from experiencing pain; rather they became a fortress for the pain that was already inside me.

Control and distrust were my coping mechanism, pillars I used to construct my emotional walls, but they were not guiding me to the results I desired. At best, they offered me temporary relief by way of denial and escapism from the reality that I needed to trust and surrender to God. Surrender requires vulnerability.

Vulnerability replaces walls with clear windows that allow people to see inside. Windows can be opened, so that the spirit of love can enter, like wind. Perhaps at some point, it's possible to reach another level of vulnerability that doesn't even require windows. True vulnerability with God has no boundaries; it is possible to be fully yourself and abide in love. But for now, when it comes to people, I've moved from walls to windows, a step closer to experiencing true love.

In college, I had a girlfriend who grew up quite differently from the way I grew up. She had both parents, lived in a nice home, ate three meals a day, and nobody ever cursed her out. One Thanksgiving, I went home with her rather than spend the holiday alone. The environment was something like scenes I had watched on television, but never experienced. Music was playing, the dining room table was covered with platters of food, and a giant turkey held center stage right in the middle of the table. Everyone laughed, kids played games, and I sat in the living room with my girlfriend's family members.

She and I sat on the couch watching the football game with her cousins, and her grandmother sat in a chair that only *she* was allowed to sit in. It was clear that I was a little different from them, but no one voiced it until my girlfriend stood up to leave the room. As she was walking, something fell out of her pocket, and I said, "You dropped something on the flo." A couple of family members grimaced, while others' eyes were wide in shock. Then my girlfriend's grandmother said to her, "Baby, did your friend just say 'flo'?"

"Grandma, please don't," my girlfriend replied.

I wasn't sure what the problem was and no one explained it to me. But I understood later. At that time I had not learned what one of my friends who's a high school principal refers to as "paycheck English." I now know that the "r" is not silent in the word "floor," and it's not proper to say "close the doe." It's "Please close the door." Nor is it "Can I have some moe?" but "**May** I have some mo**re**?"

Grammar was the least of the new skills I had to learn in being vulnerable with women, showing my true self. In the process of trying to figure out who I'm meant to be in the world, I've had to revisit a lot of old memories and experiences that hurt me deeply. I've been able to start over and build a new foundation. I've taken steps to name the pain and identify the ways in which these experiences shaped my self-esteem (or lack thereof), making me feel inadequate and insecure.

So much of my identity—beliefs about who I am—was connected to constantly being told I was stupid, to lacking self-confidence because I was bullied by my uncles, and to distrusting out of fear of emotional and physical abuse. And while I've had to calm and comfort my childhood inner wounds, I have continued to do the work of overcoming emotional wounds inflicted in my adulthood, even today. This includes allowing myself to accept my poor grammar and hood speech and finding the courage to share my feelings without fear of rejection because I don't always speak "paycheck English." Counseling, meditation, prayer, and honest conversations with friends I can trust to hold me with open hands continue to be assets on the journey.

It would be dishonest of me to say that I have completely overcome the emotional trauma related to my upbringing. I no longer have a three-second hug rule. I can handle about seven seconds now. I don't think I will ever get to twenty seconds. Just as I sometimes slide back into hood grammar, I continue to make mistakes with women. I just try not to. When I do, I seek to learn the root cause, the lesson, and try not to repeat it.

Perhaps the greatest lesson I have learned is that God can turn mistakes into miracles. Not just my mistakes but even those perpetuated by the people who were the source of my wounds. When courageously confronted, wounds become scars—the evidence of healing. As I continue to risk love by being in a relationship, I strive to reveal who I am, scars and all, knowing that it helps me love and accept myself and hoping I will be loved and accepted.

When I think about getting love right, my thoughts turn to the Bible, namely, First Corinthians. I have heard this passage of Scripture many times, but now I under-stand it in a way that is helpful to my journey of healing and self-love.

> If I give all I possess to the poor and give over my body to hardship that I may boast, but do not have love, I gain nothing. Love is patient, love is kind. It does not envy, it does not boast, it is not proud. It does not dishonor others, it is not self-seeking, it is not easily angered, it keeps no record of wrongs. Love does not de-light in evil but rejoices with the truth. It always protects, always trusts, always hopes, always perseveres. Love never fails.
>
> *1 Corinthians 13:3–8 NIV*

God is love, and now when I read these words, I some-times replace the word "love" with "God" in some sec-tions. For example, I might paraphrase it to say that *God is patient, God is kind, God is not easily angered, God keeps no record of wrongs. God does not delight in evil but rejoices with the truth. God always protects, God never fails.*

When I am struggling with self-doubt or some life-limiting belief that has crept back into my thoughts,

I meditate and replace sections of this Scripture with my name: Romal is patient, Romal is kind, Romal is not easily angered, Romal keeps no records of his own wrongs. Romal is always hopeful. Roman always perseveres. Romal does not fail but he learns from every experience.

Exchanging the words helps me get love right because I am able to refocus. I am able to remind myself of who God is in my life. *God is patient with me, kind to me, not easily angry with me, keeps no record of my wrongs and rejoices when I live in truth. God is always protecting me and will never fail me.*

I am able to love and affirm myself and refocus my attention on the kind of man I truly desire to be by saying: *I am patient with myself, kind to myself, I don't keep records of my wrongs or judge myself. I am not easily angered, I rejoice in truth, I protect myself by treating myself well. I never fail, I only learn what doesn't work, offer myself grace, and gain wisdom along the way.*

I am grateful for who I am becoming because of who God is. I am grateful for the daily opportunities to get it right. I'm grateful that God never gives up on me and I didn't give up on myself. *Love is an inside job*, and in order to get love right, I have to look inside myself, cope with what I see in the inner me, and work on healing. I have to do the work of dealing with my truth, all of it, even what I have avoided and do not love about my own story. I have to forgive myself for sacrificing the real me, and even true love, on the altar of public perception. I know, for sure, that the Spirit is forgiving.

The real you, the you that is loved and loving, the you that has moved beyond the pain of the past, is waiting for permission to be revealed in vulnerability. Your soul is yearning for a yes to love, a yes to God.

CHAPTER 11

Why I'm Here—
From Mess to Miracle

My therapist asked me, "Do you want to know the ten words at the core of your struggles?" That caught me by surprise, and fear of the answer delayed my curiosity. When he said, "You are not in control and you don't like it," I waited for twenty minutes before I actually counted the words. Therapy helped me to let go of control and embrace vulnerability.

Allison Posell, ordained minister, Aldersgate Church, Montgomery, Alabama

If you'll recall, in chapter 5, I shared what Juanita said that day we were praying in a hotel lobby in New York: "God says He had to take you this way." I've reflected on what she meant. Did God actually intend for me to go through so much verbal, emotional, and physical pain?

No. I don't believe that's what God intended. I do believe that sometimes those who are supposed to love, nurture, and protect can do us the most harm. People act on what they know, what they have learned, and can project their pain into the lives of their children. That's what I believe happened to me. Even though they did not *intend* to cause me pain. They were acting from their own hurt. God's intention is for me to be my authentic divinely created self and to find my voice and my place in the world. In all I've been through, God has been with me, showing me how to be vulnerable enough to turn pain into purpose and use it as a testimony, a story of redemption.

When I have the opportunity to share my story to help others find the courage to heal, I feel I'm making a difference. Juanita was right. God had to take me on a journey where I would remain restless until I was willing to own my truth. I had to learn how to love all of who I am and bring an end to my self-judgment. Hiding the ugly experiences and the messy mistakes, in an attempt to fit in, was suffocating. I finally had to accept and love all the parts of me. My whole self is all I have. It's my gift from the Creator. God has given me the assignment to give myself—whole, while still flawed—back to the world in ways that help others heal.

After the first talk I ever gave in a church, the pastor looked at me from the pulpit and said, "Romal, you are gifted in so many ways. There is a passage in the Bible where Jesus talks about a treasure hidden in a field. I don't have time to explain it right now but your assignment is to find that field." He was referring to Matthew 13:44. Every person is born with a gift they are here to give back to the world in ways that impact the lives of others. Like many, I have wrestled with finding my gift/ my field. For much of my life, I chose careers based on what I thought I should do in order to be respected and valued by society. I made decisions based on what would make the most money because I was afraid of being poor. I've been good at most of what I set out to do, but I would sabotage my own success because of internal demons or I would simply be unhappy.

I think what the pastor was trying to tell me is this: The only way to find the treasure hidden in the field is to cultivate the field, take care of the field. Cultivation takes time and a lot of hard work. The field is your life. You can't take care of only one area of your life; you have to care for all of it. You must pay special attention to places where you find the weeds of past pain, because when they are ignored and left untended, they spread. When you cultivate your field, you will find the hidden treasure—the reason why you are here—that allows you to flourish.

REDEEMING TRUST AND VULNERABILITY

I've set out to build healthy connections. Doing so continues to require empathy, grace, forgiveness, and most of all, love. Throughout my life, I have felt alone. At times, that loneliness has led to despair and eventually loss of the will to live. Life can feel very empty when you don't have people to share it with you. Every time I've felt alone or believed no one cared, it was of my own doing. I had no one to call when I needed a listening ear, because I wouldn't let anyone get close enough. I was afraid of being hurt, but unwilling to take the risk of vulnerability. I believed people could not be trusted.

Willingness to be vulnerable has required courage. The only way I replaced my childhood belief that people can't be trusted was to give new people a chance. I often still have to remind myself, speak to my wounded inner child, that it's safe. I have to remember that I now choose who is in my life, and the people who are in my life today have no connection to what happened growing up. Allowing myself to be vulnerable has created opportunities to let people into the places where I would normally have built a wall. It also gives me a chance to be authentic and honest rather than pretending things are okay when they're not. Pretending is a barrier to genuine relationship. It's a sign of distrust without ever giving a person the chance to show that he or she is trustworthy.

I've been quick to throw relationships away for what I felt was the slightest threat of emotional harm. If my feelings were hurt, I pushed people away. If I found out someone gossiped about me, I never spoke to that person again. I now understand that my inability to offer myself grace and forgiveness for my mistakes made it difficult to offer it to others. Walking away was easy. That didn't require any effort to try to work things out. It was also a form of control. But in many of those situations, walking away only perpetuated my internal pain and loneliness. It was self-sabotage. Living the life I truly wanted required forming new beliefs about people and a continual effort to act on those beliefs. My new beliefs are that some people *can* be trusted, do not intend to harm me, and have my best interest at heart. With time this has become easier to believe, but I still have my struggles.

Healthy relationships offer the opportunity to give and receive love. When friends draw close in times of celebration or hardship, they become evidence of what

God's love looks like in our lived experiences. My friends, who have become a part of my new narrative that is not defined by past pain, create space for me to be myself without fear of judgment. They hold me accountable and keep me honest—telling me the truth, in love—and they check in to make sure I'm doing okay. They celebrate with me in the good times and hold me with open hands during the tough times. Through relationships with loving friends, I have been able to redeem the parts of myself that childhood trauma made difficult to embrace. My friends today are a reflection of the person I am now and the kind of person I desire to become.

In his book *The Happiness Equation*, Neil Pasricha describes "The Five People Test." Look at the five people closest to you, he says, and you're the average of them. The Five People Test is one of three tests that can reveal the authentic self. When I think about the five people closest to me, they have very similar characteristics. First and foremost, they are happy. My friends enjoy life and sharing life with others. I see those qualities in myself, although I need to raise the bar on happiness sometimes because I stress out more often than I maintain a mindset of happiness. I'm glad I have my friends to balance me out. I call them my "Fave Five." All of them have positive outlooks and engage in constructive conversations instead of gossip. Even if the conversation is about something bad that happened, they don't linger on the negative. I can be overly pessimistic, but these days I find myself becoming more like my friends, having a more optimistic outlook. Most of all, my friends are loving and compassionate. They love people. Each of them is intentional about acknowledging the dignity of everyone they meet, treating them with respect, and engaging in conversations that display genuine interest. I'm glad I'm the average of my Fave Five, because I'm very much an introvert and small talk is painful to me. But the more I listen to my friends engage others, the more I realize their talk is not "small" at all. They genuinely care. They're not casual with their interest in people. I can see myself developing those qualities. A lesson I am learning from the example set by my friends is not to worry about what to say when I meet new people, but show my genuine concern for them, honor the other person's dignity, and respect his or her value.

My friends freely offer me relational gifts with every interaction. As a good friend, I strive to pay them forward. If I am the average of the five people closest to me, that makes me a pretty good person because my Fave Five are pretty amazing people! I'm blessed to call them friends.

Redemptive friendships continue to give me so much that I did not receive growing up. They give me good examples to follow, exemplify love, affirm my value, offer encouragement, and provide me honest observations that help me become a better person. And they keep me from feeling alone in the world. Friendship is indeed essential to the soul.

The lessons I've learned about friendships also inform how I relate to women. I am able to treat women with respect and operate from a place of integrity. I've learned to let go of what guided my unhealthy behaviors and emotional distance. It does not serve me well in becoming the man I desire to be in the world. I now seek to live empowered to treat women with dignity and respect. I am mindful that I have a daughter, and as a man, I am responsible for giving all women the same level of honor I want other men to extend to my daughter.

Embracing the love of God has enabled me to finally start loving myself and, in turn, love others. I no longer see women through the lens of emotional neglect that I experienced as a child. Sex is no longer only a means of receiving love, affection, and emotional connection.

I own the man I am now. I do not impose my past pain on present interactions. Women are not conquests on my troubled journey of self-validation. Women are not a means to compensate for my low self-worth. I no longer base the choice of a mate on my fractures but on who I am now and my dream of building a better future with someone I genuinely love.

In my past treatment of women, I have plenty I should be ashamed of, and I have felt shame. Taking that shame to God—being vulnerable with my Creator, Who loves me no matter what I've done—has made me fortunate enough, not only to receive God's forgiveness, but to start asking myself this question: What will you be remembered for? In trying to honestly answer that question, I admitted what I broke along the way and started cleaning up those relationships by humbly asking to be forgiven. I discovered I couldn't fix it all. That harsh reality led me to trust even more in the power of grace.

Every man seeking to become the best version of himself owes it to himself, the people he's hurt, and God to clean up his mess as best he can and live such that the man now tells a better story than who he was in the past. In order to break the cycle that perpetuates generational pain and unhealthy relationships, someone has to tell the truth. A courageous person has to confront the ghosts, the hidden stories, and bring them into the light, so that no one else has to live in the darkness of loneliness and emotional isolation.

Your story is not over, but it may be time to start a new chapter.

RECLAIMING DREAMS

I used to love drawing as a kid. I would sketch pictures to show my mom and share with classmates at school. Everyone thought I was pretty good at drawing. That changed in the sixth grade when I decided to enter a drawing contest. I sketched a picture and mailed it in. Months went by and I forgot about it. One day, when I got home from school, mixed in with mail for my mom was a letter addressed to me. I was one of the winners of the contest! I was invited to Paris to attend a gathering with other young artists and could possibly attend art school in Paris. I was excited and couldn't wait to tell my mom. When she got home, I said, "Momma, I won a drawing contest!" and showed her the letter. After reading it, she yelled at me: "Who told you to do this? I'm not letting you go to school in Paris!" Those weren't her exact words; she used a few expletives to make her point.

After my mom stopped yelling, I went to my room and cried. My sadness was not because I felt I wasn't good enough; the invitation was evidence that I was. I cried because I interpreted my mom's anger as her way of telling me *she felt* I wasn't good enough. I was a kid, and since she didn't explain her reaction, I was left to draw my own conclusions about why I could not go.

I'm sure making me feel inadequate wasn't her intent. Her anger was likely because she was afraid something would happen to me while I was gone to a place far beyond what she knew. Or maybe she feared being alone while I was away and that fear of loneliness came out as anger. Maybe she was afraid that she would have to pay for it and knew we didn't have the money. Whatever her reasons for yelling at me, that moment took away my desire to draw. I never drew anything again.

I've revisited many of the scenes that were the source of my emotional pain, some so deeply repressed that I forgot they even happened. I don't like revisiting the pain of the past, because when I think about what happened to me, it still hurts. But I take the emotional journey back in time, so that it stops hurting once and for all. I confront, feel, and name the pain. I feel it one last time, identify what that experience took from me, and then reclaim it.

This is inner work, an inside job. It isn't engaging in looking back at negativity. It's learning from the past and reinterpreting it through the lens of time and who I am now. It's examining my experiences and their impact on me, redeeming my self-confidence and self-worth, and regaining the courage to try without fear of failure. From this process, I affirm that I am capable, know that I am lovable and able to love. It's courageously embracing the fact that I am fearfully and wonderfully made just the way I am because I was created by an amazing God (see Psalm 139:14).

Love is an inside job means doing the work to become the real me that was lost to an outdated story of my past. That story created life-limiting beliefs that did not serve me well in creating a life of meaning filled with love.

A major part of my inner work includes reclaiming my dreams. With so many disappointing life experiences, I stopped dreaming. I was afraid to dream because life had taught me that they probably wouldn't come true. I would rather stick with the pain I knew than risk encountering pain I did not know. I focused on how I would feel if things went wrong. I wouldn't let myself imagine how amazing I'd feel if they worked out the way that I desired. My dreams were deferred and, in the words of Langston Hughes, left to "dry up like a raisin in the sun."

Today, I love collecting art. My first piece was a Charles Bibbs limited edition print he titled *A Mother's Love*. I bought it while in college because it reminded me of my grandmother. I had four roommates and didn't have any place to hang it, so it sat on the floor next to the television in our room. I'd look at it every day and it would remind me of how I wanted to make my grandmother proud. Today, work allows me opportunities to travel the world, and whenever I'm in other countries for work or pleasure, I buy art. Pieces from South Africa, Kenya, Thailand, Brazil, Colombia, Cuba, India, and many other places hang in my home. I've even started creating an inventory of art and jewelry in preparation for my dream of owning an art gallery.

When asked, "When did you first realize you loved art?" the question suddenly brought to memory winning that art contest. I realized I loved art since I was a kid, but that experience took it from me. That letter affirmed art as something special for me, and when I shared that letter with my mom, a dream died. In revisiting the pain of what happened, I've been able to reclaim what it took from me and live my dreams. I'm no longer a child powerless to make my own decisions, but a capable adult who is able to keep dreaming in spite of adversity. No one's words get to decide my future. That day, when my mother yelled at me for trying, was a moment in my life, but I cannot let it determine the rest of my life.

My love of art is no longer a dream deferred. I dream and work to make my dreams come true. I didn't make that trip to Paris when I was a kid, but today I get to travel the world collecting art. No longer a dream deferred, my love of art is a dream redeemed.

WHAT WILL PEOPLE THINK?

A recent conversation with a friend went something like this:

"Hey, Romal, it's been a long time. Congratulations on your next book. I follow you on social media, and from the looks of things, you seem happy in all of your photos."

"Thank you. It's true. I'm not just Facebook social media happy, but I'm real-life happy. I love my life."

"Ha! That's great. So glad your appearance of happiness is legit!"

Five years ago I lost a job, and another relationship with the woman in my life was ending. It was a really tough time, but I wanted to convey a message through the social media world that I was happy. I wanted the people who knew the challenges I was facing and followed me on Instagram and Facebook to see that I was not hurt by the difficulties in my life. But I was. I was downright miserable. Yet I still smiled for the cameras and pretended that life was okay.

Back then I was so unhappy that I resented people who shared their successes, vacations, celebrations, and so on. I went as far as un-friending them. My insecurities and personal struggles would not allow me to celebrate another's success. I wish I could have seen the victories of others as a sign of hope during my low moments. That would have been a motivation that life can and will get better, an emotionally healthy and positive approach to take. Instead, I continued to put on the façade of Facebook happy while scrolling and resenting the pictures and messages posted by others.

The person I had become was not based on my truth but on my desire to be accepted and wanted. Rather than being myself, I was what I thought other people wanted me to be. My assumption was that if they knew the real me, they wouldn't want me. I never gave them a chance to meet the real me. I had not accepted myself. My career, where I lived, the car I drove, the people I knew, and the clothes I wore were all based on what I wanted people to think about me—on wanting to be liked. My thinking had been that people would value me and treat me like I mattered if I had all the right things. And it worked—but only to an extent. As long as people were telling me how well I performed and how nice the things I owned were, I felt good about myself. The downside was that it became addictive. Just thinking about the amount of money I wasted buying stuff that I thought would make me "somebody" makes me want to kick myself now. I could be financially wealthy now if I hadn't spent money trying to buy something that couldn't be purchased: my own self-worth and internal value.

I've always craved praise. But no amount of praise could fill the void in my soul. I had to be doing something or accomplishing something that would cause people to tell me how good I was. It was like a gas tank with a hole in it—except the hole was in my soul. No matter how much people fueled my need for validation, my tank emptied quickly and I longed for more fuel (praise). If I wasn't "busy," I felt useless, like I didn't matter.

I had to find value within myself before anyone else could affirm it. I had to know that I mattered for no other reason than the fact that I am human and my life has value. How I felt about myself was an inside job and not something other people could give me. They could affirm me, but they did not have the power to define me. The people around me did not create me, so they could not tell me what I was created for.

I am not the only one who has put on an appearance of truly enjoying life to cover up for sadness, disappointment, or uncertainty about the future. If, like me, you gather your composure, take a deep breath, and smile for the camera, pretending to be happy but empty on the inside, ask, as I did: Why do I do this? Why do I pretend? Why am I so compelled to present a false reality?

"Fake it until you make it" may work when pursuing a career, but it is a terrible way to deal with your emotional life. It does not allow you to have the normal and natural human experience of feeling what you need to feel in order to be patient with yourself without judgment and go through the process of finding balance again. Pretending only prolongs the process, dulls the pain of disappointment, and does not exempt us from having to eventually deal with the source of the problem.

So why did I fake it? Why do any of us fake it and pretend to be Facebook happy? We have been conditioned to believe that public perception is more important than the truth. We fear that true happiness is elusive or unrealistic. I am not suggesting you tell the world your problems on social media. Most of us cringe when we see that. It is *social* media, not personal life media. Some things are better *off* the Internet. But what other people thought of me became more important than what I actually thought of myself. If people liked me, then I would like myself more. (I literally counted the number of people who clicked "Like.") If the world thinks I am happy, maybe one day I will actually be happy. Too many of us are sacrificing happiness and fulfillment for the sake of appearances.

Five years ago, I was officially burned out from putting on the façade and pretending for the sake of public perception. However, I was so conditioned to live my life based on what I wanted other people to think that I did not know how to stop myself. I went to dinners that I did not want to attend because of what other people would think if I did not show up. I went to meetings for so-called important leaders because of what I wanted other people to think. I said yes to things I did not want to do and to people I did not like out of fear of shaming. Meanwhile I felt guilty because deep down I knew I wanted to say no. I was a professional people pleaser who specialized in the art of public perception. I was miserable, so I called my therapist to help me sort through all the foolishness.

I developed a strategy for focusing on honoring the love of God and love for myself. These are the questions I asked: What are your reasons for sacrificing genuine happiness on the altar of public perception? Who would you be and what would you do if you stopped worrying about what other people think? What benefit do you get from compromising who you are for the sake of what other people think? Has that benefit ever really delivered as you hoped? My answer to every question was no.

It's very hard to enjoy life when you are more concerned with public perception than your own happiness. I've stayed in unhealthy relationships and people have stayed in unhealthy relationships with me because we were worried about what other people would think. Both of us sacrificed the possibility of finding true love or genuine friendships on the altar of public perception. At times I was afraid to leave a job that I didn't find fulfilling; I endured because I was worried about what other people would think if I chose a more fulfilling career that was less glamorous or "successful." I was sacrificing purpose, fulfillment, and meaning on the altar of public perception. Like many others, I have remained silent while "friends" or colleagues gossiped about others who were not present because I was afraid to speak up in fear of being rejected. As a result, I sacrificed my character and values on the altar of public perception.

One of the best lessons I learned from my therapist, Warren, is that "The greatest form of betrayal is self-betrayal." I betray myself when I compromise my values for the sake of public perception and worry about what other people think. Every choice I make will either enhance my sense of self or cause me to betray myself. A key to self-love is doing my best not to betray my heart, the essence of who I am.

I do, of course, care about what *some* people think. In a video, Brené Brown said she carries a one-inch by one-inch slip of paper with the names of every person in her life whose opinion actually matters. I follow her example. I have thousands of social media friends but only eight people on my one-inch by one-inch slip of paper whose opinions actually matter to me.

Perhaps like me, you need to take full ownership of your life and stop living like a character trapped in someone else's play, letting public perception choreograph your decisions. It is your life. You get to write the script *and* play the lead. The saying "You only live once" is not true. As I learned from my friend Shaun, "You only *die* once. You live every day."

I can honestly say that today I am truly happy, genuinely happy, even unapologetically happy. I've learned to embrace the love of God, and I know how to love myself. I still have moments of difficulty and disappointment. My happiness is rooted in a healthy perspective about who I desire to be in the world that keeps me focusing on meaning and expressing daily gratitude.

You are already *amazing*. You do not have to prove that, and you do not have to pretend. You just have to believe it and live like it.

MY PAIN CONTAINED THE ROAD MAP TO MY PURPOSE

My education, the people I came to know, the dinners and meetings I was invited to, and the things I owned aren't what make me feel important. It is my story. My painful past story has created opportunities for me to dream big and see the world, by sharing my truth. My story gives people permission to share theirs, too, and stop hiding in shame.

Some stories in my life I wanted to forget and pretend did not happen. The stories I wanted to hide were the stories God was asking me to reveal so the Almighty could heal me and use me to heal others. Confronting and healing those parts of my story that I didn't like have become the key to true emotional freedom and the ability to love all of me without shame or guilt. Those moments I wanted to forget were taking power from me to be myself, and I wanted that power back. Words were said that hurt me, and things were done that bruised me, but none of it had the right to define me.

When I thought about my life as a story, it was easy to focus on the good things that happened, the encouragement I received, the experiences that made me feel good about myself. But I forgot other stories, buried them. Some I never told. Others I wanted to forget or tried to cover up. The tragedy, for me, was when I chose to hide my scars, I hid the evidence of healing. In hiding my pain, I hid my growth, hid it from myself, from others, and from those who have suffered the same wounds, so I couldn't be a resource to help them. My scars—my hidden stories—were the evidence of possible healing for them. My buried stories were God's testimony to the world. I am modern-day evidence of what God is doing in the world today. Testimony is the evidence of truth. My life is evidence that while potentially tragic events occur, God's healing cannot be denied.

Sharing my own truth—what I had kept hidden from the world—was liberating. Owning my truth—naming my wounds—continues to be a tool for my healing and a guide for helping others do the same thing. I don't simply show my wounds; that's not helpful to anyone. When we only show people our wounds, we just bleed all over everybody. No, I want to also show how I turned those wounds into scars. Scars become the evidence to others that healing is possible.

I have found my truth and my true self. I am no longer ashamed of parts of me, but instead I am learning how to love all of me. Lying beneath what I had long thought was the rubble of my childhood pain, I have found my purpose and who I am meant to be in the world.

A PLACE TO BELONG

My relationship with God has still not always been easy. At times, I find myself angry with God. At other times, I experience deep feelings of gratitude and love that literally overwhelm me. I've learned that in every moment, every circumstance, God is always present and always waiting to be embraced. Nothing can separate me from God's love. I was created by God's love. The fact that I am here is evidence of God's love. Those who love me are the embodiment of what God's love looks like. To live in this unlimited love requires only a simple yes to God.

One of the greatest desires of my heart has been finding a place to belong, to find my tribe, the people who I can relate to and live in community with. My greatest barrier to creating or becoming a part of community has been my inability to be still. Since childhood, I moved a lot: different schools, different communities, and new friends every year. I never maintained connections with friends I left behind. Back then, we moved out of necessity; we couldn't afford to pay the bills. As an adult, I have moved and disconnected myself from friends constantly to prevent being hurt and rejected. I was unwilling to let people get too close.

The more I understand the importance of relationships, the more I find myself cultivating community. I love traveling the world and meeting new people. But travel does not mean the absence of a place called home. Community is connection, a place to love and be loved, to support and encourage, while receiving the same in return.

Community, for someone like me who travels frequently, is like Indy 500 auto racing. Drivers race at high speeds for miles, but at some point they have to stop and see the pit crew. Pit stops are a very dynamic and fast-paced process where everyone is working simultaneously. The driver does not always stop because something is wrong; sometimes a driver checks in and makes sure everything is okay. The pit is critical to success. When the driver takes the car off the track, it is swarmed by eleven to twelve people cleaning the windshield, adjusting the mirrors, changing the tires, refueling the car, and most important, making sure the driver is okay. A loving community is life's pit crew. Community is the place where people play important roles in the races of our lives, and we also do so for them. Everyone in community is both driver and crew. We clean off each other's windshield by making sure we have the right perspective on life. We adjust each other's mirrors by challenging motives so that we avoid blind spots. We change the tires and fill the tank by giving each other love, affection, and words of affirmation, so we know we are loved and valued whether we win or lose the race.

I've finally found my tribe, my community, my pit crew. The community I have is not one where we all live in the same neighborhood or even the same city. I have what I come to define as an itinerant community. Traveling and meeting new friends have allowed me to develop friendships with people across the country and even other parts of the world. My Fave Five live in Washington, D.C., Chicago, and Los Angeles. They are friends who have become like family to me. I can call them under any circumstances. They come to see me and I visit them. I used to believe that I would only have peace once I found a place to call home, with all the people I love together. But I've learned that peace of mind is like love—it's an inside job.

A BANQUET OF GRACE

The pain caused by my mom and dad made me feel like I was a character trapped in a play produced by my parents. I wanted to hide parts of the story, and other parts I didn't want to admit even existed. One day while attending a retreat in Florida, I had the opportunity to share with a friend how my relationships with my parents caused me to feel pain and shame. After listening to me, Stan shared a powerful story.

"We don't get to exfoliate any parts of our lives. When I became forty-six, I did not leave forty-five behind. But the experience of forty-five came with me. Our lives are like the concentric circles of a tree. When you cut a tree in half, you see the circles that represent the tree's growth. They are all part of the tree. All of your life's experiences are part of you, even the parts you don't like.

"But every day you prepare yourself for a banquet of grace. And at this banquet, the present you—the person with agency and wisdom from the lessons learned—sits at the head of the table. At this banquet are all of the memories and things that you like about yourself: the accomplishments, positive experiences, and victories you've won. Everything good about you is seated at the banquet table. But standing outside in the cold and rain with their faces pressed against the window are the parts of you that you don't like: the disappointments, the mistreatment, the failures, the abuse—and they want a seat at the banquet, too. So you let them in.

"But the present you sits at the head of the table. Not the fearful ten-year-old, the insecure eighteen-year-old, or the uncertain twenty-two-year-old. The present you sits at the head of the table but offers grace to all of you."

I keep offering myself grace because the story is not over, and neither is yours.

Steps for Vulnerability with God

Love of God > Self-Love > Love of Others

REMEMBER HONESTLY

Remember your story, recall your past—the parts that make you feel good and those that do not.

BE AWARE

Observe your behavior while in the act of doing what you don't want to do, without judging yourself.

ACKNOWLEDGE

Call your behavior what it is, rather than ignoring it. (I didn't understand the difference between awareness and acknowledgment, and my therapist, Warren, explained, "Awareness is like being in the grocery store and seeing someone you know. If you avoid talking to them because you don't want to be bothered, you are aware of that person but you chose not to acknowledge them. Acknowledgment is going over and speaking to the person.") Accept the reality of your behavior and what you are doing and name it.

AFFIRM

Offer yourself grace. You are not your behavior. You are not the emotions attached to your behavior. You are a child of the Divine. God made you and loves you unconditionally. Brutal honesty must be connected to relentless grace. There is no healing without grace. Grace is at the core of forgiving and healing.

CULTIVATE GRATITUDE

Be grateful. The mere fact that you want to be better and desire vulnerability is progress.

ADAPT

After accepting who you are—God's creation—and what you are doing, identify ways you will adjust your behavior. Plan ways you will respond differently the next time you find yourself in a situation where you can be vulnerable instead of behaving the way you have in the past.

This is a continuous process. I know I will inevitably make mistakes, but I stay in the process of choosing vulnerability over my past behaviors. Over time, I know it will not be as difficult, but the process will never end.

Love requires vulnerability, and I want love like I want the air I breathe. Sometimes my life experiences make it hard to even know what loves feels, looks, or sounds like. The amazing thing about God's love is that I experience it even though I don't have everything figured out. God's love does not require perfection; it only requires the desire to receive it and say yes to it. For most of my life I thought I had to fight for everything that I wanted. Now I realize that fighting was not what I needed to do because the battle is not mine, it's the Lord's. God has been waiting for me to surrender.

Group Guide

Turn your suffering into grace; otherwise it's just wasted pain. It's your job to transform from your pain.

Elizabeth Gilbert

INTRODUCTION. TO LOVE THY NEIGHBOR AS THYSELF, GET VULNERABLE WITH GOD

1. Think of someone you felt was trying to please God but was actually just pleasing other people. How are you able to tell the difference?
2. Recall a time when you found yourself trying to earn the love of God by pursuing the validation of people.
3. Do you have difficult life experiences that you have not let God into?

Receiving God's love means being vulnerable with God. Loving God means being vulnerable with God.

CHAPTER 1. "WHEN THE PARTS OF ME I DIDN'T LOVE LED A REVOLT…"

1. The mistake I have made that I find most difficult to accept is _____.
2. The hurt I have experienced that has been most difficult to accept is _____.
3. When _____ happened, I just tried to forget it ever happened in order to "move on."
4. Because of the mistake, the hurt, or what happened, I probably responded to the situation with [name another person] in an unhealthy way. Talk about that situation.

I cannot change the things that have happened, but I can change the story that I have been telling myself about me because of what happened.

CHAPTER 2. THE VERDICT WAS THERAPY

1. Name three negative beliefs about therapy that you've heard.
2. Whom would you *not* tell you were going to therapy?

3. Whom could you tell you were going to therapy who would not see it as a sign of weakness?
4. Whom could you tell you were going to therapy who would ask, "Is something wrong with you?"
5. Name an individual who would understand how therapy might be helpful to your emotional health and wellness.

I have pretended to be happy, pretended that I enjoyed life, but now I actually want to become the person I have pretended to be. Some part of me now cares more about having peace than maintaining the perception that I am in control.

CHAPTER 3. HAUNTED BY THE PAST

1. Write down a past pain in your life for which you're still waiting for an apology.
2. Now, write down the words "I'm sorry" as if they were coming from the other person, and write the words you want to hear from that person that would allow you to heal and let go of your past pain.
3. What negative and painful events from your past still affect you, and how would your life

today be so much better if they had never happened?

4. Describe who you would be today if you no longer defined yourself by what happened back then.

I don't need to hold today accountable to what happened yesterday. In the present moment, I have the right to choose my path and understand myself differently in light of what happened back then.

CHAPTER 4. CHANGE IS A CONTACT SPORT

1. Recall a time you found it hard to accept the love and support of others.
2. Every family has its stories. Share a favorite positive story from your past.
3. Every family has its stories of wounds. Reflect on one that you do not want to discuss or think about.
4. Are you able to pinpoint ways the difficulties in your family story influence how you live your life today?
5. Which of the stories I shared about how therapy helped me to revisit my past did you most relate to?
6. Is there value for you in seeing someone to help you

figure out what you need to do differently in order to break a family cycle of pain?

Love is an inside job means doing the inner work of healing emotional wounds and becoming who you are truly meant to be.

CHAPTER 5. WHO'S LOOKING FOR ME?

1. Describe an instance where God used you to let people who do not go to church know that they are still loved and valued.
2. What can you do differently as a Christian that would reflect God's love toward people who do not go to church?
3. Reflect on a situation in your life when a stranger displayed generosity, encouraging words, or an act of kindness toward you. How was that evidence of God's love for you?

God has always been looking for me. When I was down and God wanted to encourage me, God used the voices of men and women to inspire me. When I needed to know that I was loved, God used the arms of compassionate people to console me.

CHAPTER 6. CHURCH HURT

1. Think about the life that you have been trying to create for yourself and identify one instance when you have engaged in "self-sabotage."

2. Name an area of your life where you have been trying to control the outcomes.

3. In what area of your life have you trusted God with the outcomes?

4. Everyone has a "church hurt" or negative experience with organized religion. What's yours?

5. What are some characteristics of people who make it difficult for you to be a part of a worshipping community?

6. If you no longer saw church through the lens of who you were at the time you were hurt, but based on who you are now (empowered through experience and wisdom), what might you do differently?

7. Tell someone your "church hurt" story and discuss what would allow you to forgive people in the church.

8. If you could make up the perfect church, describe what it would look like: how people are treated, how they're supported, and what you would do as a member of that kind of church community.

9. Would that church still be perfect when you became a part of it?

10. I can engage the church in a more positive way by _____.

Rather than seeing the church through the lens of who I was in the past, I have to re-enter the story based on my spiritual growth, as the person I am now. I am no longer the same person I was when I was first introduced to organized religion. I can now have a different church experience because I have the wisdom of experience and the insight of lessons learned from my own mistakes.

CHAPTER 7. VULNERABLE WITH GOD AS FATHER AND HONEST WITH MY DAD

1. Does my relationship, or lack thereof, with my father help me feel God is a loving Father?

2. Is God less about love and more about punishment?

3. Is God only proud of me when I am achieving?

4. Does God love me because He created me?

5. Does forgiveness have most to do with the other person?

6. Is forgiveness releasing myself from carrying the weight of past pain?

7. Is forgiveness letting the other person off the hook for their behavior?

8. Is forgiveness letting myself off the hook for someone else's actions?

9. What do you need to forgive your father for?

10. What does your father need to forgive you for?

11. Name a positive aspect of your behavior that you picked up from your father.

12. Name a negative aspect of your behavior that you picked up from your father.

13. What can you do differently to break the pattern?

14. Write your dad a letter, based on who you are now, not who you were as a child.

I impose on God the experiences I've had with people—perhaps my father. When I attempted to be vulnerable, I was hurt in the process. I realize the difference now: God is love. Not sometimes, but all the time. God doesn't turn love on and off. God doesn't have issues like my parents. God isn't carrying any emotional baggage. God can always be trusted. I know, for sure, that God's Spirit is forgiving.

CHAPTER 8. MEN FRIENDS—THE THREE-SECOND RULE

1. Recall some experiences from your childhood that make receiving affection easy or challenging.
2. When I think of the word "affection," I think _____.
3. I could receive affection more freely if _____.
4. More people have gone through physical abuse than care to admit. Those experiences make giving and receiving affection challenging. At the same time, all of us as human beings need affection. List three ways you can help a survivor of abuse feel safe receiving affection from you.
5. If you are a survivor of abuse, describe what would make you feel safer when receiving affection.
6. How could therapy help?

Vulnerability can be terrifying. It opens the door to be hurt. But it also offers the opportunity to love and be loved. Vulnerability is the freedom to feel deeply and have empathy. Vulnerability allows me to receive the comfort and security that comes with knowing I am deeply loved and cared for without an agenda.

CHAPTER 9. BROKEN MEN

1. As children, boys are not often nurtured to become vulnerable men. Describe a scene to show what it would look like to model vulnerability as strength rather than a weakness.

2. In what settings (places and environments) could we teach male children the power of vulnerability to help them become emotionally healthy men?

3. If we stop telling boys not to express their feelings, what would we have to *start* saying?

4. What new things would you explain to them about crying, sadness, and affection?

5. It's easy to think about the people who hurt you in life and feel you deserve an apology for their actions, but it's another thing to realize that you may be the source of someone's else's pain. Inasmuch as you have felt the need for an apology, there are people who need an apology from you. Name three people who need to hear you say, "I'm sorry."

6. How would you offer them the same kind of healing that you desire for yourself?

7. Write a letter to someone that you have hurt.

I will not use the fact that I was broken or hurting as a cop-out for my bad behavior. I own my bad behavior and admit that those I hurt deserve an apology. I am courageous enough to go back and revisit the pain I caused them and offer them what they need for healing.

CHAPTER 10. BADGES AND BURDENS

1. Recall a secret in your family that is a source of sorrow.
2. Recall a secret that might be keeping you from living your desired life.
3. In total private, tell God about your secret.
4. In your private conversation with God, ask for strength to do whatever you need to do to be freed from your secret.
5. What would it take for you to have inner peace and joy if you could never buy another thing?
6. What belief would you need to change about life in order to be content with your life as it is right now?
7. Name some positive habits or ways of being in intimate relationships or marriage that you saw modeled growing up.
8. What one behavior and way of being in intimate

relationships learned from your family needs to change?

9. What do you need to do differently to make that change?

10. Name a relationship benefit you would reap from that change.

I have to do the work of dealing with my truth, all of it, even what I have avoided and do not love about my own story. I have to forgive myself for sacrificing the real me, and even true love, on the altar of public perception.

CHAPTER 11. WHY I'M HERE— FROM MESS TO MIRACLE

1. Explain how a testimony differs from a complaint or pity party.

2. Tell someone a part of your story, your past pain, that you have not been willing to share, offering it as a tool to help someone else overcome a similar challenge. (Keep in mind that to be a tool, it must have a positive outcome and path to healing.)

3. What belief about people needs to change in order for you to live the life you truly want?

4. What belief about life needs to change in order for you to have the types of relationships you truly desire?

5. What belief about friendship needs to change in order for you to have the types of relationships you truly desire?

6. What beliefs about you and your past need to change in order for you to have the types of relationships you truly desire?

7. Make a list of your five closest friends and their characteristics. What do those characteristics tell you about yourself based on the kinds of people you have in your life?

8. Remember a goal or a dream that you did not pursue because of something someone said or did.

9. What would you have to do to redeem your dream?

10. In the words of my therapist, Warren, "The greatest form of betrayal is self-betrayal." What is one way you have betrayed yourself because you were worried about public perception, what other people would think?

11. What would you need to do differently in order not to betray yourself?

12. Write down life limiting beliefs, caused by your past, that need to be released in order to live the

life that you truly desire. Now tear the paper to smithereens.

13. What is the biggest outside factor keeping you from getting the emotional help you need to sort through painful life experiences and beliefs that are no longer useful to you?

14. What is your biggest inner resistance to getting the emotional help you need to sort through painful life experiences and beliefs that are no longer useful to you?

15. What part of your story do you sense God has been calling you to heal?

16. How would getting vulnerable with God and honest about your story help you embrace love and support more freely?

17. Pray, in your own words, a prayer that admits you want to be vulnerable with God and experience emotional freedom. Be sure to ask God to, "Show me how to love all of who I am without shame or guilt."

Love is an inside job means becoming the real me, including the inner me that was lost to an outdated story of my past. That story created life-limiting beliefs that do not serve me well in creating a life of meaning filled with love.

Acknowledgments

Aman Victoria Tune

Jordan Romal Tune

Dorothy Molex (my mom, 1952–2006)

Jeannette Felder-Molex (my grandmother, 1921–2003)

William Molex, Sr. (my grandfather, 1923–1989)

Gary Tune (my dad)

Marchet Sparks

Joseph W. Daniels

Rudy and Juanita Rasmus

Christian Washington

Warren Mitchell (my therapist)

Konyia Clark

Adrianne Sears

Tashion Macon

Robert Lee

Lisa Grant-Dawson

Sheila Bates

Courtland Wyatt

John Herring

Larry Sampson

Ned and Barbara Simmons

Edward Simmons

Richard Rohr

Sherry Bailey

Grace Tweedy Johnson

Don Jacobson

Philipia Hillman

Robert Lee

Adrienne Ingrum

Blair Jacobson

About the Author

Romal Tune is senior advisor to the president of TMS Global, while also maintaining his public relations consulting company, Tune & Associates. He is a highly sought-after communicator and seminar facilitator. His platform and cross-sector relationships have positioned him as a global leader who takes individuals and institutions from setbacks to success by using the power of story. Romal constantly travels throughout the year, helping individuals and organizations find deeper meaning, maximize their potential, and live into their purpose by listening to their stories and living authentically. Coming from challenging beginnings, Romal defied the odds to become an All-American Collegiate Scholar, Who's Who in American Colleges and Universities, and magna cum laude honor graduate with a BSN from Howard

University and an MDIV from Duke University School of Divinity. As a military veteran who served during Gulf War Desert Storm, Romal knows full well about moving individuals from setbacks to success as leaders.